54-

The New York Times

IN THE HEADLINES

Consumer Culture

FEEDING CAPITALISM

THE NEW YORK TIMES EDITORIAL STAFF

Published in 2020 by New York Times Educational Publishing
in association with The Rosen Publishing Group, Inc.
29 East 21st Street, New York, NY 10010

First Edition

The New York Times
Caroline Que: Editorial Director, Book Development
Phyllis Collazo: Photo Rights/Permissions Editor
Heidi Giovine: Administrative Manager

Rosen Publishing
Megan Kellerman: Managing Editor
Julia Bosson: Editor
Greg Tucker: Creative Director   AUG 1 4 2020
Brian Garvey: Art Director

Cataloging-in-Publication Data
Names: New York Times Company.
Title: Consumer culture: feeding capitalism / edited by the New
York Times editorial staff.
Description: New York : The New York Times Educational
Publishing, 2020. | Series: In the headlines | Includes glossary
and index.
Identifiers: ISBN 9781642823547 (library bound) | ISBN
9781642823530 (pbk.) | ISBN 9781642823554 (ebook)
Subjects: LCSH: Consumer behavior—Juvenile literature. |
Consumption (Economics)—Juvenile literature. | Consumer
goods—Juvenile literature. | Popular culture—Marketing—
Juvenile literature.
Classification: LCC HF5415.32 C66 2020 | DDC 658.8'342—dc23

Manufactured in the United States of America

On the cover: Companies try to lock people into buying their
products without comparison shopping; Brian Britigan/The New
York Times.

Contents

CHAPTER 4

Consumer Behaviors

CHAPTER 5

Critiquing Consumerism

Introduction

IN 1939, PRESIDENT Franklin D. Roosevelt announced that Thanksgiving would be celebrated a week earlier that year. The calendar had the holiday falling on the last day of November, leading retailers to claim they would not have enough time before Christmas to hold their sales. Roosevelt listened.

This decision demonstrated the unique link between American culture and consumerism. Each holiday celebrated in America has its connections to material goods of some kind: Thanksgiving has Black Friday; Valentine's Day its Hallmark cards and heart-shaped boxes of chocolate; Christmas and the gifts that accompany it. America is the home of Amazon, big box stores and, of course, the shopping mall, the site of so many movies and television programs. No newspaper or magazine in America exists without a large advertising section. Culturally speaking, consumerism is as American as apple pie (which can be purchased at just about every grocery store nationwide).

The articles in this collection seek to untangle and examine particular aspects of consumer culture, considering both its workings as well as its implications. In these chapters, journalists reckon with the ways in which consumerism has become a pernicious and enduring aspect of American culture as well as the ways it has helped boost the economy. They explore how consumerism impacts psychology and the various methods retailers use in order to predict and capitalize on consumer behaviors. In several articles, journalists explore the relationship between supply and demand as merchandisers play a cat-and-mouse-game with consumers, attempting to predict trends even as consumers dictate the flow of capital.

MICHAEL WARAKSA

As technology has evolved, so too have consumer patterns. Over the last twenty years, mom-and-pop stores were largely eradicated by the rise of centralized shopping malls and big box stores such as Walmart and Target. More recently, the unprecedented rise of Amazon, which has transformed from a book merchandiser to an online behemoth that sells everything from toilet paper to on-demand television, has changed the game, leaving many shopping malls ghost towns and major retail chains struggling to stay afloat.

There has also been a series of public exhortations to make consumerism a more conscious aspect of American life. As the link between consumption and climate change has become more clear, there has been a rise in the zero-waste movement, which attempts to eliminate waste and to only use products that are recyclable. And as Americans have seen money and power consolidated in the hands of corporations and executives, there have been moves to help protect the individual consumer, including the Consumer Financial Protection Bureau, which was created in 2011 under a plan by Massachusetts Senator Elizabeth Warren.

As buying largely shifts online, new models of retail are being created. In some places, while larger department stores have closed, small businesses have cropped up, offering a more curated consumer experience. And now that our phones have become the primary medium through which we engage with the world around us, it stands to reason that they will impact the future of consumerism in America.

The buying and selling of data in order to create more and more targeted advertisements has become the financial backbone of the tech world. Facebook and Google make their fortunes by delivering promotions directly intended to attract their users. Soon, geotracking will be used to encourage consumers to visit stores as they pass them. As the economy evolves, what the tech companies need is for consumers to continue with what they do best: consume.

CHAPTER 1

The Culture of Consumerism

Over the course of the 20th century, consumerism has become an integral part of American culture. The production of and mindset behind the purchasing of material goods is so deeply ingrained that it constitutes an identity. The articles in this section explore the various manifestations of consumer culture, ranging from individual acquisition habits to those great beacons of consumption, shopping malls.

In Buying We Trust: The Foundation of U.S. Consumerism Was Laid in the 18th Century

BY PAUL LEWIS | MAY 30, 1998

"A PENNY SAVED is a penny earned" and Benjamin Franklin's other homespun exhortations may stir nostalgia for an earlier age when habits of frugality and thrift are thought to have been more deeply ingrained in the American character.

Yet some scholars have questioned whether those early colonial Americans wouldn't have been almost as devoted to, say, the Home Shopping Network as their modern counterparts are.

"Recent scholarship has convincingly demolished the notion of a sudden and late revolution that transformed America into a nation of consumers," writes Daniel Horowitz in "The Morality of Spending," a 1992 history of consumer attitudes. Carole Shammas, a historian at the University of California at Riverside, agrees: "The foundations of American consumerism were laid in the 18th century," when large quantities of imported manufactured goods from England started to circulate in the 13 colonies.

Indeed, the origins of colonial America's relationship with thrift and consumerism are complicated. While there was certainly a reverence for the values associated with thrift, there was also a vital and active consumerism.

Yet until recently, only the thrift side of the equation was emphasized. It was assumed that thrift was an article of faith for America's early Protestant dissenters, Puritans, Baptists, Methodists, Quakers and the like. And indeed, they believed that God had called man to occupy a particular place in this world, and therefore he must fulfill the obligations imposed on him by his "calling." This implied careful husbandry of possessions because they came from God.

As David Fischer, a historian at Brandeis University, points out, as late as 1775 no less than three-quarters of the churches in the colonies belonged to dissenting Protestant faiths that believed every man had such a sacred calling.

Many colonial Americans also harbored a visceral suspicion of wealth, luxury and self-indulgence, believing they threatened social cohesion. When James Oglethorpe was planning the settlement of Georgia, for instance, he envisioned a utopian society in which each family would be limited to 500 acres and trade in land would be prohibited.

But the picture of the self-sufficient early settler carving a home out of the wilderness in a pre-capitalist environment is only part of the story. Historians now argue that thrift was imposed on the early colonists by the natural rigors of the world they found and for many reflected not so much a monkish wish to live simply as the desire to grow richer.

As John Wesley, the 18th-century founder of Methodism, wrote, "We ought not to prevent people from being diligent and frugal; we must exhort all Christians to gain all they can, and to save all they can; that is, in effect, to grow rich."

And Alexis de Tocqueville, the celebrated French observer of the New World, noted in 1831 that "Love of money is either the chief or a secondary motive at the bottom of everything the Americans do."

Max Weber put another dent in the thrift myth more than 50 years ago in his famous work "The Protestant Ethic and the Spirit of Capitalism." He showed how belief in salvation through hard work at one's "calling" laid the foundations of capitalism by encouraging men to accumulate riches. Such accumulation was fine in the eyes of the early American Protestants as long as men resisted the temptations that the riches created. Thus what Weber termed the "worldly asceticism" of America's Puritan founders also contained the seeds of that rip-roaring modern consumer capitalism that was eventually to devour it.

These days many historians believe early American colonists were even more involved in a market economy than previously thought, importing goods from England and trading with each other rather than fighting what one historian has termed "a desperate rear-guard action against the spread of capitalism."

In a paper titled "An Empire of Goods," the historian T. H. Green said that Staffordshire china was the 18th-century equivalent of Coca-Cola.

And in "Wealth of a Nation to Be: The American Colonies on the Eve of the Revolution," Alice H. Jones writes of "the substantial size and character of wealth in consumer goods" among colonists.

In fact, historians such as Shammas, Jones and Horowitz argue that the continual exhortations to be thrifty and practice self-restraint were prompted by the growth of consumerism, not the lack of it. Americans throughout the 18th century and even more in the 19th were faced with a growing array of consumer goods such as glass and china, pots and pans and decorative objects, making frugality a difficult virtue to embrace.

From 1828 to 1878, Sarah Hale, a famously prolific journalist, preached the virtues of thrift to American housewives in women's journals and tirelessly inveighed against consumption. These years saw the establishment of over 600 savings banks in the Eastern states by philanthropic bodies such as the New York Society for the Prevention of Pauperism and The Christian Disciple, a Boston religious paper, with the express aim of encouraging thrift among the working poor as well as savings institutions in public schools to teach children thrifty habits.

At around the turn of the century the intellectual climate shifted with the emergence of three thinkers who predicted an age of economic abundance in which the need to preach thriftiness would no longer be appropriate.

In "The New Basis of Civilization," published in 1907, Simon N. Patten saw the United States moving from "a pain or deficit economy" to a "pleasure or surplus economy." His conclusion, eerily similar to that reached by John Kenneth Galbraith 50 years later in "The Affluent Society," was that the country's surplus should be used to help the poor and to improve public services, not on conspicuous consumption by the rich.

Thorstein Veblen, who coined the phrase "conspicuous consumption" in 1899, also understood modern industry's potential for raising living standards across the board but carped at the rich for diverting its product to their own extravagant uses. The lesser-known George Gunton, a British immigrant, preached that shorter working hours and high wages stimulated mass consumption, profiting worker and capitalist alike.

With the American entry into World War I, the Federal Government threw its weight behind a national thrift campaign to pay for the conflict, selling $17 billion worth of Liberty Bonds and collecting $1 billion in War Savings. So successful was this campaign that Treasury Secretary Andrew Mellon tried to continue it after the peace but ran into significant opposition from business, which, with industrial productivity rising, wanted people to spend.

In New York, store windows were plastered with posters of Uncle Sam at the controls of a locomotive saying: "Full speed ahead. Clear the track for prosperity. Buy what you need now." Even The New York Times called the Government's thrift campaign irritating and wearisome. In 1924 the United States Treasury threw in the towel. Officially sanctioned consumerism had won.

Only after the World War I did the golden age of mass consumption first envisaged by Patten, Veblen and Gunton finally dawn.

In "Buy Now, Pay Later" published in 1991, Martha L. Olney says the 1920's saw a revolution in consumer taste as Americans not only increased their purchases of consumer durables but also switched from buying china, furniture, books and jewelry to newly mass-produced items such as cars, radios and household appliances.

The average American household spent $79 a year between 1889 and 1908 on consumer durables; that rose to to $267 a year from 1919 to 1928, helped by the invention of consumer credit and an explosion of advertising spending that was deductible from the excess-profits tax imposed on business in 1917.

Since then thrift has taken a backseat to American consumerism. Some intellectuals have seen the shift as an encouraging sign: In 1954 David M. Potter argued in "People of Plenty" that the country's economy of abundance had shaped its view of democracy, freedom and equality by encouraging leveling up instead of leveling down.

Today thrift and mass consumption appear incompatible. Big-spending America has long had one of the lowest rates of savings in the industrial world and last year it fell further, to 3.8 percent of average household income from 4.3 percent the year before.

In classical economic theory, low savings leads to less investment and industrial weakness. But now a revisionist school of economists led by Martin Feldstein at Harvard and Paul David at Stanford argue that buying a car or a home is like an investment because it brings long-term benefits over time, just as spending on education should be considered an investment because it increases earning power. If such spending is included, then the country's savings rate has been running at over 25 percent throughout the century, Professor David calculates.

It may be that thrift and consumerism are compatible after all.

Spend, Spend, Spend.
It's the American Way.

COLUMN | BY ROBERT J. SHILLER | JAN. 14, 2012

The Economic View column explores life through an economic lens with leading economists and writers.

GRIDLOCK IN CONGRESS implies that there won't be any collective decision to spend more as a nation to get out of our slump. Increases in deficit spending seem unlikely, and so does the balanced-budget stimulus I've been advocating in this column. For now, we must pin our hopes for a robust recovery on the willingness of millions of consumers to spend substantially more.

But what really drives consumer spending? Economists are reasonably good at divining how consumers tend to react to changes in government policy, but in the absence of such policy, and when the economy is in the doldrums, they aren't very good at predicting spending shifts.

A new book, "Beyond Our Means: Why America Spends While the World Saves" (Princeton University Press), offers some insights. It was written by Sheldon Garon, a Princeton professor who is not an economist but rather a historian with a sociological bent.

Professor Garon says that our willingness to spend is driven most prominently by our reaction to major events in our collective memory, including wars and depressions, and that it also depends on national character, which differs across countries and through time. Spending, of course, is shaped by deliberate government policies. Notably, during wartime, governments all over the world often start huge public-information campaigns to promote saving.

The United States, however, is something of an exception. More than any other country, Professor Garon argues, it elevates consumer spending to a virtue, sometimes minimizing saving. There is even an idea here that it is patriotic to spend, rather than to save.

For example, in a speech two weeks after the Sept. 11 terrorist attacks, President George W. Bush urged Americans not to be cowed: "Get down to Disney World in Florida," he declared. "Take your families and enjoy life, the way we want it to be enjoyed." Personal consumption expenditures increased sharply in October 2001, and the recession that had begun in March of that year came to an abrupt end by November.

In more recent times, many parallels have been drawn to the Great Depression. Presidents and prime ministers worldwide justified their stimulus packages in 2008 and 2009, for example, by saying that if these plans weren't put in place, we might repeat the economic nightmare of the 1930s. That kind of talk might have been necessary to assure support for stimulus, but it certainly hurt confidence.

And there was another problem. The truth is that stimulus packages never entirely lifted the economy out of the Great Depression. In the United States, unemployment didn't drop below 12 percent until World War II changed the picture.

In recent months, news that Christmas shopping appeared strong, at least soon after Thanksgiving, was invested with great significance. Holiday cheer, it was argued, might provide the needed stimulus. But this is an old story. In every Christmas season of the decade-long Great Depression, newspapers described a strong, even frenzied, Christmas shopping season.

Perhaps this offers a lesson in bias. It seems that during such bad times even the most respectable newspapers somehow needed to write an upbeat story for the holidays. Confidence-building is part of our culture, and it helps to explain confidence swings.

During the Depression, George Gallup began to compute confidence indexes. But sharp improvements in confidence, as reported in 1938 by Gallup's American Institute of Public Opinion, did not spell the Depression's end. Eventually, consumer demand did come roaring back — after World War II, contrary to economists' widespread fears that the Depression would resume after the war.

Professor Garon details an attitude that Americans, more than people in any other country, have usually had about spending: we tend to think it's O.K. for people to go into debt to buy gadgets or take vacations. According to this view, such activity will stimulate everyone's imaginations, and ensure a vibrant economy with plenty of fresh enterprises and innovations. Americans even tend to think that debt burdens may not be so bad — that people in debt work harder to pay it off, again keeping the economic engine humming. We are relatively forgiving of personal bankruptcies, too: they provide a fresh start to allow spending all over again.

In much of the rest of the world, Professor Garon documents, this approach has traditionally seemed morally repugnant — though until the current crisis, many people worldwide were slowly coming around to the American view.

Governments around the globe have long promoted pro-saving — that is, anti-spending — campaigns. Professor Garon notes that many of these campaigns flourished during wars, when frugality was a necessity to conserve resources. In World War I and World War II, government campaigns left a lasting impression that overspending was immoral and unpatriotic, and for most countries the campaigns did not stop when the wars ended.

The United States had such savings-promotion campaigns during those wars, too, but it gradually ended them afterward. By 1966, the United States had suspended its postal savings system — which encouraged savings by allowing people to buy certificates of deposit at post offices for as little as a dollar. Many countries still have such systems, as part of efforts to make saving seem convenient and patriotic.

Low consumer confidence during the Depression could have been caused partly by fear of war, many commentators said at the time. But it is hard to measure the validity of such claims.

In any case, fear of war doesn't seem the main problem today, despite some unease about possible crises in places like Iran and North Korea. In the United States, there is concern about the economic stability of Europe, but barring a major collapse there, it is likely to remain a distant worry.

Patriotism may turn out to be a stronger force here. The killing of Osama bin Laden last year will probably be recounted over and over in this year's election campaign, which, like many campaigns before it, is certain to be filled with patriotic rhetoric. But would a patriotic surge change the mood enough for consumers to take personal risks to get on with the American Dream?

While these kinds of mental and moral factors are very hard for economists to evaluate, they may be all-important for the current outlook.

ROBERT J. SHILLER is professor of economics and finance at Yale.

You Can't Take It With You, but You Still Want More

BY MATT RICHTEL | JAN. 4, 2014

ALL WORK AND NO PLAY may just be a result of "mindless accumulation."

So say scholars behind research, published in the journal Psychological Science in June, that shows a deeply rooted instinct to earn more than can possibly be consumed, even when this imbalance makes us unhappy.

Given how many people struggle to make ends meet, this may seem a frivolous problem. Nonetheless, the researchers note that productivity rates have risen, which theoretically lets many people be just as comfortable as previous generations while working less. Yet they choose not to.

To explore the powerful lure of material accumulation, the researchers constructed an experiment in two phases. In the first phase, subjects sat for five minutes in front of a computer wearing a headset, and had the choice of listening to pleasant music or to obnoxious-sounding white noise.

They were told they could earn pieces of Dove chocolate when they listened to the white noise a certain number of times. Some participants had to listen fewer times to get each piece of chocolate, making them "high earners"; some had to listen more times, making them "low earners."

All were told that there would be a second phase to the experiment, also lasting five minutes, in which they could eat the chocolate they earned. But they were told they would forfeit any chocolate they couldn't consume, and they were asked how much they expected to be able to eat.

On average, people in the high-earner group predicted that they could consume 3.75 chocolates.

But when it came time to "earn" chocolates, they accumulated well beyond their estimate. On average, they listened to enough white noise to earn 10.74 chocolates. Then they actually ate less than half of that amount.

In other words, they subjected themselves to harsh noise to earn more than they could consume, or predicted they could consume.

"We introduce the concept of 'mindless accumulation,' " said one of the paper's authors, Christopher Hsee, a professor of behavioral science and marketing at the University of Chicago Booth School of Business. "It's a waste of effort," he added. "But once people are in action, they can't stop."

The impulse seemed less pronounced, even mixed, with the low earners. They earned less chocolate than they predicted they could eat. But the high earners and the low earners listened to about the same amount of obnoxious noise in the five-minute period, which Dr. Hsee said strongly suggested that both groups were driven by the same thing: not by how much they need, but by how much work they could withstand.

How applicable is this to the real world, where people earn money, not chocolate, and can't predict how long life will last, or whether they will need resources to prepare for a calamity? Hard to say, but the study does show that even when people know clear boundaries — that they absolutely can't take the candy with them when they go — they still earn more than they can possibly use.

Michael Norton, an associate professor at the Harvard Business School who is familiar with the field, said the study's implications were "enormous" in part because they can enlighten people to an unconscious motivation that leads to shortsighted, even unhappy choices.

Still, he said, choosing happiness or leisure over earning is challenging, in part because accumulation of money — or candy — is easier to measure than, say, happiness. "You can count Hershey's Kisses," Dr. Norton said. Being an involved parent or partner is not so quantifiable. "Most of the things that truly make us happy in life are harder to count," he said.

Joy to the Packaging People

OPINION | BY GARY S. CROSS | DEC. 12, 2014

WE ARE ENTERING a season of packages, of wrapped and packed commodities, that many of us rewrap in colorful paper and ribbons to present as holiday gifts. Thus we disguise the mass-produced, try to effect an aura of mystery and magic, and hope our gifts fulfill, or even awaken, the desires of their receivers, with the latest "must-have" toy or fashion. This really curious habit has been common in the United States and elsewhere for over a century. In fact, it closely parallels the advent of packed and wrapped goods for daily use.

Think of Coca-Cola, that drink many people once recognized by its distinctive green bottle, and now recognize as much by its red-and-white can as by its caramel-colored caffeinated sugar kick. Since the 1890s, Coca-Cola has been replacing milk, fruit juice and water in the diets of millions of people around the globe. Coca-Cola is only one of hundreds of new commodities, engineering and marketing feats, that have liberated us from the limits of nature, for both good and ill.

If, as often told, we humans are makers (Homo faber), we are also packagers, and have been since the ancients first poured wine into colorful amphorae. We wrap the stuff of nature (foods, drinks, but also sights, sounds and other sensual pleasures) in skins that entice, but that can also deceive us, much like the holiday gift box. By the 1880s, merchandisers learned that the boxing, bottling and labeling of often quite ordinary bulk foods and drinks not only made for personal portable convenience (as in that Coke can or box of Cracker Jack), but that the labeling with colorful logos coordinated with massive advertising in magazines, newspapers and on billboards created special meanings that made the ordinary extraordinary, almost like the beribboned gift. This has been the hallmark of the twin occupations of the merchandiser and the advertiser ever since. From childhood, we are trained to long for the wrapping as much as for what's inside, just as kids are taught to believe that the wrapped toys under the Christmas tree come from Santa, not Wal-Mart.

But what's inside is not just chopped liver (usually). We try to pack as well as to wrap, like holiday gifts, besting the ordinary. Thus we preserve food and drink that would otherwise easily spoil in sealed pots, and since the 19th century, in metal cans. We try to improve on nature by besting its ephemerality and seasonality. Packaged food and drink have eliminated the need for the traditional harvest festival as a time for feasting on soon-to-spoil fruits and vegetables, and on the pork and beef from domesticated animals that could not be fed through winter. With packing, we have it all whenever we want, whatever we want.

Yet the packing means much more. It has long been about intensifying sensation: turning sweet grape juice into psychotropic wine. And that quest to pack more punch into nature's delights has exploded in modern times with the extraordinary concoctions invented toward the end of the 19th century. Think of Jell-O, little more than powdered gelatin made from animal byproducts and enhanced with sugar and flavoring that from 1897, through advertising, but also through the appeal of convenience and the delight of its jiggle, won over mothers and especially their children, supplanting all-American apple pie. Every industrial society has some variety of these concoctions (say, the Anglo-Australian yeast spread Marmite/Vegemite or Scotland's soft drink Irn-Bru, both acquired tastes). One of the most successful of these repackaged natural products is, of course, the cigarette, the dark side of modern packaging.

The packed and the wrapped extend beyond the sense of taste, including efforts to capture, preserve and often to duplicate the ephemerality of sight, sound and even touch. Although drawing and painting were attempts to possess the visual, it was the arrival of the camera (1839) and the motion picture (1891) that created the fixed and the flickering image; these were amazing feats that both displaced and perpetuated vision. And the phonograph (invented in 1877, made practical starting in 1887) magically captured voice on the continuous groove of a cylinder or disc.

These devices created what no painting or sheet music could: an exact and seemingly infinite reproduction of images and sounds, accessible anytime, anywhere. And, as we all know, these technologies soon repacked sight and sound, creating experiences of surprising intensity.

Note the accelerated pace of the quick-cut film (as in "The Great Train Robbery" of 1903). This technique was endlessly copied and refined in action pictures since the 1970s, from "Dirty Harry" to "The Lego Movie."

The packed and preserved sensations of film and vinyl were often enhanced by wrappings: enticing motion picture posters and trailers, as well as record sleeves with provocative images on the front and "liner notes" on the back. The image of the Beatles on the psychedelic-themed album cover for Sgt. Pepper's Lonely Hearts Club Band (1967) is iconic and perhaps as memorable as the songs themselves.

Thus, it's both the external wrapping and the internal packing that make packaged commodities what they are today. Lately these principles have been applied with renewed vigor: consider the current wave of new "foods" manufactured from vegetable proteins and engineered to taste like meat (Tofurky and Soyrizo), or the shift from physical movies, records or books to the streamed digital song or e-book. This swing from the physical/tactile to the virtual has been sweeping and sudden, but this new product is still a package.

Yet, these seemingly unstoppable trends are inevitably met by packaging luddites. These are people who still favor the old packaging — vinyl records or CDs that can and must be stored, displayed and ritualistically set up for play; and bound paper books that take up space on shelves and tell you and your friends something about who you are or were. There are still those who insist on nature's original wrapping, like bananas that can be peeled, and who value the process of selecting, cleaning and cooking fresh vegetables for stir fry. Some people may even reconsider those piles of presents and opt for other ways of sharing and celebrating the winter solstice.

We are a packaging people as we once again prepare for the gift season. Optimally, we can both enjoy the benefits of packaging and continue to embrace ephemeral and intermittent natural pleasures. Need the one completely supplant the other?

GARY S. CROSS is a professor of history at Pennsylvania State University, and one the authors, along with Robert N. Proctor, of "Packaged Pleasures: How Technology and Marketing Revolutionized Desire."

Should You Have Things?

OPINION | BY ANNA NORTH | DEC. 15, 2014

"TO CARE ABOUT POSSESSIONS can seem like a moral failing," writes Julie Beck at The Atlantic. "The holiday season especially can make people ornery about 'stuff' and the companies that encourage us to buy it."

It may not be just the season. Minimalism is trendy, even (or perhaps especially) for those who could afford to be maximalist. And research suggesting you should spend your money on experiences rather than on things is on its way to becoming conventional wisdom. One recent proponent of the experiences-versus-things ethos is Leslie Bradshaw, who writes at Medium:

> Young people have redefined success, and their new definition values experience over possession. The word 'experience' may sound like a code word for 'free,' but the change is not necessarily a reaction to underemployment or even a desire to save money.

Rather, she says, choosing to own few things "allows for much more flexibility — financially, geographically, spatially, liquidity'ly." And she cites a story by James Hamblin, in The Atlantic, about the happiness-boosting powers of experiences.

"Even a bad experience becomes a good story," writes Dr. Hamblin, reporting on research by Matthew Killingsworth, Thomas Gilovich and Amit Kumar. "When it rains through a beach vacation, as Kumar put it, 'People will say, well, you know, we stayed in and we played board games and it was a great family bonding experience or something.' Even if it was negative in the moment, it becomes positive after the fact. That's a lot harder to do with material purchases because they're right there in front of you."

Ms. Beck, though, cites some evidence in favor of things. "Rather than serving as a poor substitute for human connection," she writes, "it would seem that objects can amplify those connections." And she talks to Maryam Afshar, who has studied attachment to objects and notes that even a refrigerator can have value to someone beyond its intended purpose: "Say the refrigerator was owned by someone's mother who passed away recently, and now she gets to have the one that her mom was using in the past few years."

"In that case," Ms. Beck writes, "the fridge isn't just utilitarian, and isn't as replaceable." Ms. Beck also relays what happened when, as research for the book "The Meaning of Things," the psychology professor Mihaly Csikszentmihalyi and his co-author Eugene Rochberg-Halton asked a Chicago widow which of her possessions were special to her:

> She immediately stood up and took them to the bathroom, where she opened the vanity over the sink to reveal a shaving brush and a razor. They belonged to her husband, who had passed away several years before. From there, she showed the researchers photos of her children and grandchildren, and Christmas presents she'd received the year before.

"It has been an important experience to see how people can take ordinary things and transform them into meaningful symbols," Dr. Csikszentmihalyi tells Ms. Beck. "We can create aesthetic experiences — not only aesthetic, but ecstatic — by paying attention to what's around us, finding the beauty in things that you normally pass over."

Dr. Hamblin writes about the possibility of "making purchasing an experience," perhaps by "buying something on a special occasion or on vacation or while wearing a truly unique hat. Or tying that purchase to subsequent social interaction." But by Dr. Csikszentmihalyi's logic, people are already turning their things into experiences, sometimes simply by recalling the connection between those things and people they love.

Ms. Beck also writes, referring to the work of the marketing professor Russell Belk, that "the loss of possessions, ones deeply associated with the self, can cause real grief."

At The New Yorker, Allen Kurzweil writes about one such possession — an Omega Seamaster watch that had belonged to his father,
who died when he was 5. The watch fell victim, he believes, to the influence of his boarding-school bully, Cesar Augusto Viana:

> *Within the week, his henchman admitted that he'd hurled my watch*
> *off a balcony on a dare. I ran down the stairs, dashed outside, and*
> *dug through knee-deep snow until my fingers turned white and tingly.*
> *The watch never surfaced. The loss left me more than bereft. I felt*
> *annihilated.*

Much later, after he's confronted Mr. Viana as an adult, Mr. Kurzweil realizes: "My father's Omega turned out to be more than a talis-
man. It was a time machine that had transported me back to a moment
when my family was intact and I was happy." And, he writes:

> *When I told my wife and son that I was banishing Cesar from our lives,*
> *they celebrated his eviction by giving me an extravagant gift. I am wear-*
> *ing it on my wrist.*

Experiences, good or bad, may become stories, but Mr. Kurzweil's account — and, to an extent, that of the widow in Chicago — suggests that things may have a narrative power, too. They may help us tell the stories of our lives, of what we've lost and what we've gained.

ANNA NORTH is an Op-Ed columnist for The New York Times.

The Economics (and Nostalgia) of Dead Malls

BY NELSON D. SCHWARTZ | JAN. 3, 2015

OWINGS MILLS, MD. — Inside the gleaming mall here on the Sunday before Christmas, just one thing was missing: shoppers.

The upbeat music of "Jingle Bell Rock" bounced off the tiles, and the smell of teriyaki chicken drifted from the food court, but only a handful of stores were open at the sprawling enclosed shopping center. A few visitors walked down the long hallways and peered through locked metal gates into vacant spaces once home to retailers like H&M, Wet Seal and Kay Jewelers.

"It's depressing," Jill Kalata, 46, said as she tried on a few of the last sneakers for sale at the Athlete's Foot, scheduled to close in a few weeks. "This place used to be packed. And Christmas, the lines were out the door. Now I'm surprised anything is still open."

The Owings Mills Mall is poised to join a growing number of what real estate professionals, architects, urban planners and Internet enthusiasts term "dead malls." Since 2010, more than two dozen enclosed shopping malls have been closed, and an additional 60 are on the brink, according to Green Street Advisors, which tracks the mall industry.

Premature obituaries for the shopping mall have been appearing since the late 1990s, but the reality today is more nuanced, reflecting broader trends remaking the American economy. With income inequality continuing to widen, high-end malls are thriving, even as stolid retail chains like Sears, Kmart and J. C. Penney falter, taking the middle- and working-class malls they anchored with them.

"It is very much a haves and have-nots situation," said D. J. Busch, a senior analyst at Green Street. Affluent Americans "will keep going to Short Hills Mall in New Jersey or other properties aimed at the top 5 or 10 percent of consumers. But there's been very little income growth in the belly of the economy."

Once a thriving mall, Rolling Acres in Akron, Ohio, is now a crumbling reminder of better days. Since 2010, more than two dozen enclosed shopping malls have been shuttered, and 60 more are on the brink, an analyst says.

At Owings Mills, J. C. Penney and Macy's are hanging on, but other midtier emporiums like Sears, Lord & Taylor, and the regional department store chain Boscov's have all come and gone as anchors.

Having opened in 1986 with a renovation in 1998, Owings Mills is young for a dying mall. And while its locale may have contributed to its demise, other forces played a crucial role, too, like changing shopping habits and demographics, experts say.

"I have no doubt some malls will survive, but major segments of our society have gotten sick of them," said Mark Hinshaw, a Seattle architect, urban planner and author.

One factor many shoppers blame for the decline of malls — online shopping — is having only a small effect, experts say. Less than 10 percent of retail sales take place online, and those sales tend to hit big-box stores harder, rather than the fashion chains and other specialty retailers in enclosed malls.

The Landover Mall in Maryland was torn down in 2006, leaving empty parking lots and one stand-alone Sears, which closed in early 2014.

Instead, the fundamental problem for malls is a glut of stores in many parts of the country, the result of a long boom in building retail space of all kinds.

"We are extremely over-retailed," said Christopher Zahas, a real estate economist and urban planner in Portland, Ore. "Filling a million square feet is a tall order."

Like beached whales, dead malls draw fascination as well as dismay. There is a popular website devoted to the phenomenon — deadmalls.com — and it has also become something of a cultural meme, with one particularly spooky scene in the movie "Gone Girl" set in a dead mall.

"Everybody has memories from childhood of going to the mall," said Jack Thomas, 26, one of three partners who run the site in their spare time. "Nobody ever thinks a mall is going to up and die."

Well aware of the cultural dimensions, as well as the economic stakes, the industry is trying to turn around public perception of these monuments to America's favorite pastime: shopping.

In August, the International Council of Shopping Centers, a trade group based in New York for the shopping center industry, including mall owners, hired the public relations firm Burson-Marsteller "to put the real story out there and stop the negativity around the idea that the mall isn't going to exist in the next few years," said Jesse Tron, communications director for the trade group.

While it is true that many thriving malls will continue to flourish in the years ahead, it is not clear what the industry can do to prevent more and more malls from falling on hard times.

About 80 percent of the country's 1,200 malls are considered healthy, reporting vacancy rates of 10 percent or less. But that compares with 94 percent in 2006, according to CoStar Group, a leading provider of data for the real estate industry.

MATT ROTH FOR THE NEW YORK TIMES

The Lord & Taylor store, which remains open and is attached to the White Flint Mall, still has some mannequins.

Nearly 15 percent are 10 to 40 percent vacant, up from 5 percent in 2006. And 3.4 percent — representing more than 30 million square feet — are more than 40 percent empty, a threshold that signals the beginning of what Mr. Busch of Green Street calls "the death spiral."

Industry executives freely admit that the mall business has undergone a profound bifurcation since the recession.

"You see the A-rated malls, the flagship malls, performing very well," said Steven Lowy, co-chief executive of Westfield Corporation, which has its roots in Australia but is now a major global player among mall owners. In the United States, Westfield has shed properties in the Midwest while focusing on the more affluent coasts. In Europe, Mr. Lowy prefers wealthy urban centers like London and Milan.

"Our business is more regional and high-end focused," he said. "There are gradients of dead or dying or flat, but anything that's caught in the middle of the market is problematic."

Tom Simmons, who oversees the mid-Atlantic shopping center division of Kimco, another real estate giant, is more blunt. "There are B and C malls in tertiary markets that are dinosaurs and will likely die," he said, but "A malls are doing well."

But there is a fuzzy line among the categories. White Flint Mall, a once-upscale destination in the affluent Washington suburb of North Bethesda, Md., is now sealed and awaiting demolition. A half-hour's drive to the east, in the economically and ethnically diverse Prince George's County, the Landover Mall was torn down in 2006, leaving empty parking lots and one stand-alone Sears, which closed in early 2014.

Both properties belong to the Lerner family of Washington, who are also the majority owners of the Washington Nationals baseball team. Lerner Enterprises has said it wants to redevelop both sites, but there are few signs of it in evidence.

Outside Akron, Ohio, the Rolling Acres mall has defied every attempt to redevelop it and now sits forlorn, with boarded-up windows and trees growing through cracks in the concrete. Before it was sealed, squatters occupied it and vandals pilfered copper wire for scrap.

When it was thriving, "people would come from all over in busloads," said Timothy A. Dimoff, a retired Akron detective who once advised on security at Rolling Acres. "Everybody in Akron still talks about the caramel popcorn in the food court."

Owings Mills may be on the verge of becoming a dead mall, but it is not in a dead-end market.

The original owner of Owings Mills, General Growth Properties, sold a 50 percent stake to Mr. Simmons's company in 2011, and now Kimco is working to redevelop it into a hybrid of an open-air shopping center and enclosed mall.

Resurrecting a dead mall isn't an easy process, however. Demolition of the old Owings Mills and construction of what is known in the industry as a "power center," with big-box stores like Costco, Best Buy and Target, would cost $75 million to $100 million and take two to five years, Mr. Simmons said. He expects Owings Mills to persist in its current, zombielike state at least through the end of 2015.

Its demise, he said, was primarily because shoppers were drawn to other properties nearby like the more upscale Towson Town Center. Although Owings Mills was originally designed as a luxury property, the mall found it harder to compete after Saks Fifth Avenue closed its anchor department store there in the mid-1990s.

"The mall genie was out of the bottle," Mr. Simmons said, "and it was never going to come back."

Unequal, Yet Happy

OPINION | BY STEVEN QUARTZ AND ANETTE ASP | APRIL 11, 2015

THE GAPING INEQUALITY of America's first Gilded Age generated strong emotions. It produced social reformers like Jane Addams, anarchist agitators like Emma Goldman, labor leaders like Eugene V. Debs and Progressive politicians like Theodore Roosevelt. By the 1920s, sweeping legislation regulating food and drugs and breaking up corrupt trusts had been passed. The road to the New Deal was paved.

But our current Gilded Age has been greeted with relative complacency. Despite soaring inequality, worsened by the Great Recession, and recent grumbling about the 1 percent, Americans remain fairly happy. All of the wage gains since the downturn ended in 2009 have essentially gone to the top 1 percent, yet the proportion of Americans who say they are "thriving" has actually increased. So-called happiness inequality — the proportion of Americans who are either especially miserable or especially joyful — hit a 40-year low in 2010 by some measures. Men have historically been less happy than women, but that gap has disappeared. Whites have historically been happier than nonwhites, but that gap has narrowed, too.

In fact, American happiness has not only stayed steady, but converged, since wages began stagnating in the mid-1970s. This is puzzling. It does not conform with economic theories that compare happiness to envy, and emphasize the impact of relative income for happiness — how we compare with the Joneses.

In the late 1800s, Thorstein Veblen, the theorist of "conspicuous consumption," proposed that jewels and mansions were little more than the human equivalent of the peacock's tail — their main purpose was simply to outdo other peacock tails.

In 1974, the economist Richard A. Easterlin famously wrote that although richer people were happier than poorer people in the same country, people in wealthier countries were not necessarily happier than those in poorer ones (once basic needs are met). More recently, the economist Robert H. Frank has described a status drive that traps Americans in an irrational consumer arms race, in which we vie for status through ever more wasteful purchases.

But if happiness depends on status, and if status depends on relative income, wouldn't today's historic income inequality predict a giant happiness gap? Why hasn't this happened?

There's no denying that socioeconomic status is still a strong predictor of social status. And class lines have become hardened. But in its cultural expression — and therefore in its effects on our happiness — inequality is increasingly disorganized. Consumerism has expanded the lifestyles, niches and brands that supply the statuses we seek.

As a result, social status, which was once hierarchical and zero-sum, has become more fragmented, pluralistic and subjective. The relationship between relative income and relative status, which used to be straightforward, has gotten much more complex.

For most of human history, inequality of wealth meant inequality of happiness. Status, and its related activities, envy and emulation, drove consumption. By the 1950s, rapidly rising standards of living across the West, combined with social pressures to conform, all conspired to intensify status competition. The architects of "rebel cool," like Jack Kerouac and Norman Mailer, responded by rebelling against emulation consumption and the status hierarchy of postwar America. They inverted the dominant social hierarchy, rejecting the values of those at the top and appropriating the values of those who had been marginalized at the bottom.

The pursuit of "the cool," in our view, fundamentally altered the psychological motivations underlying our consumer choices. In conspicuous consumption, our emulation of higher-ups means we compete directly for status because we want what they have. But rebellious consumption changed the game, by making a product's worth depend on how it embodied values that rejected a dominant group's status.

Take the Schott Perfecto leather motorcycle jacket. Worn by James Dean, and by Marlon Brando's character in the 1953 film "The Wild One," it symbolized a rejection of traditional respectability. In our time, the business suit remains the standard uniform in corridors of power in Wall Street and Washington. But in the San Francisco Bay Area, it might suggest a back-office support professional (accountant, lawyer, etc.) who serves at the whim of a T-shirt-and-hoodie-wearing tech entrepreneur and his similarly clad software developers.

There's no longer any one way to keep up with the Joneses. If the Joneses drive a BMW 3 Series, you can compete by buying a BMW 4 Series. But if the Joneses drive a minivan, you can drive a sport utility vehicle to rebel against their staid domesticity. (This is what happened in the 1990s, when suburbanites embraced the S.U.V. as a symbol of fun and adventure.) And if the Joneses drive an S.U.V., you can drive a Prius, or forgo a car altogether — as a sign that you embrace a green lifestyle.

By comparing a PC user to an Orwellian drone while likening a Mac user to a sexy athlete in its iconic "1984" ad, Apple made a fundamental claim about the allure of its products. Today, Apple products are expensive because they're seen as cool; they're not cool because they're expensive (which is still the case for many luxury goods).

A new neuroscience of consumer behavior reinforces our argument. In one experiment, we used functional magnetic resonance imaging (fMRI) to understand our brains' reaction to perceived coolness. We selected students from the Art Center College of Design in Pasadena, Calif., and asked them to rate, from uncool to cool, hundreds of images from the following categories: bottled water, shoes, perfumes, handbags, watches, cars, chairs, personal electronics and sunglasses. We also included images of celebrities (actors and musicians). The cooler objects typically weren't the more expensive ones: our subjects rated a Kia hatchback above a Buick sedan, for example.

We then asked other students to look at images of these objects and people on a screen above their eyes, while in an fMRI scanner. The most striking finding: Asking people merely to look at products and people they considered "cool" sparked a pattern of brain activation in the medial prefrontal cortex — a part of the brain that is involved in daydreaming, planning and ruminating — similar to what happens when people receive praise. Our brain's medial prefrontal cortex, in short, tracks our social esteem.

A new generation of ethnographers has discovered an explosion of consumer lifestyles and product diversification in recent decades. From evangelical Christian Harley-Davidson owners, who huddle together around a motorcycle's radio listening to a service on Sunday mornings, to lifestyles organized around musical tastes, from the solidarity of punk rockers to yoga gatherings, from meditation retreats to book clubs, we use products to create and experience community. These communities often represent a consumer micro-culture, a "brand community," or tribe, with its own values and norms about status.

Among the millennials (generally defined as those born between 1981 and 1997) the diversity of status-seeking has been especially pronounced. Studies have found that teenagers and young people in their

20s commonly use musical taste as an indicator of their identity and values. No doubt, these tastes are also shaped by ethnicity and class. Nonetheless the variety of possible identities is striking. While the top 1 percent of songs each year account for something like 75 percent of all artist revenues, there are 43 million songs for sale currently in the iTunes store.

This trade-off comes at a political price, as it makes income inequality less emotionally salient. In a 2013 poll asking Americans to name the most important problems facing the country, only 5 percent cited income inequality or concerns about the poor or middle class (though a recent Gallup poll did find that 67 percent of Americans were dissatisfied with the current income distribution). Politicians from Senator Elizabeth Warren on the left to Representative Paul D. Ryan on the right are talking about inequality, but President Obama has lately been talking more about "opportunity."

The neuroscience of consumerism doesn't exonerate our political and economic systems for the chasm of inequality that defines contemporary America. When a group feels unfairly deprived of material wealth, respect, rights or freedoms relative to other groups, that relative deprivation mobilizes political action. The proliferation of consumer choice helps explain why today's Gilded Age hasn't sparked as much outrage as the last one. Money may not buy happiness in the long run, but consumer choice has gone a long way in keeping most Americans reasonably content, even if they shouldn't be.

STEVEN QUARTZ, a professor of philosophy and neuroscience at the California Institute of Technology, and ANETTE ASP, a political scientist, are the authors of "Cool: How the Brain's Hidden Quest for Cool Drives Our Economy and Shapes Our World."

Walmart Can't Escape Clutter. Can You?

OPINION | BY PACO UNDERHILL | DEC. 19, 2015

TO THE DISMAY of economists and retailers, the American consumer keeps holding back.

Consumer spending this fall has barely budged upward and many store chains are struggling with low sales and falling stock prices. The reluctance to spend might be a result of general skittishness or a residual fear left over from the Great Recession. Or perhaps, inspired by books like the No. 1 best seller "The Life-Changing Magic of Tidying Up: The Japanese Art of Decluttering and Organizing," Americans are striving to lead simpler, more spiritual lives, free of the stuff and clutter filling up their homes and lives.

They won't find much Zen at the mall, where stores are cluttered with merchandise and promotions like never before.

There is a basic rule of thumb in retail: The more stuff in the aisle and the more promotional the environment, the higher the sales. Traditionally, the American consumer is very willing to put up with crowded aisles and a certain level of physical discomfort to find something at a good price, or a perceived one. The more crowded, the greater the reward for "treasure hunting" shoppers looking for an elusive bargain. Dollar Stores, TJ Maxx, some of us might even remember the original Filene's Basement — all thrived on their customers' sense of discovery.

In supermarkets and big-box stores, the strategic placement of goods is essential in building incremental sales. The origins of the "stack it high and watch it fly" mentality come from the way goods were originally brought into big-box stores: via forklift. As a result, the aspirational spaces we all long for in our homes — clean, uncluttered, perhaps with a few white phalaenopsis orchids sprinkled around — are completely at odds with the stores we shop in.

That chaos or in-store clutter is symptomatic of the broader questions retail is facing. After a decade of declining sales and inspired by the success of the austere Apple stores, some retailers now believe that consumers are more likely to purchase when presented with a cleaner experience and fewer options. Cluttered stores may seem more likely to hold bargains but they also appear cheaper in the minds of many consumers. Big-box stores with lots of promotional offerings are finding that customers pick something up as they move through the store and then discard it later on as they find something else they like better. So that while clutter does increase sales, it also increases labor costs as stores have to keep returning this merchandise to the right place in the store.

The question is, what is the line between a store offering stuff to be "discovered" and a plain unattractive store that just looks bad?

As it turns out, it's hard for stores to rid themselves of clutter. It's easier for brand stores like H&M, Apple or Bose to be organized because they have one brand to sell, rather than competing brands and displays. In general merchandise stores like Macy's, Target or Walmart, the displays and space in the aisle are contracted out. Pepsi, Coke and Mars may have all purchased floor space in the same quarter, and the store manager has a duty to make them all successful.

In 2009, the management of Walmart, the world's biggest retailer by revenue, decided it needed less cluttered-looking stores, so it cleaned out its aisles, lowered its shelving, and tried to streamline its merchandise and in-store promotions. They were wrong. In the stores that tried the cleanup, sales declined, resulting in more than $1 billion in lost revenue, according to one industry estimate. Stuff went back into the aisle and sales went back up. (Undeterred, Walmart is trying again.) In 2012, Ron Johnson, a retail veteran of Target and Apple, tried to streamline the stores of J. C. Penney and to cut back on the promotional price cuts. Sales dropped 25 percent, and Mr. Johnson was out of a job the next year.

Why didn't these efforts succeed? Consumers, as it turns out, are not so easy to figure out. If you ask customers if they think stores are too cluttered, the answer is a predictable yes. The problem is with the research methodology. Rather than just ask shoppers what they think they would like, I can follow someone through their shopping trip in a grocery or mass merchandise store like Walmart and Sam's Club and then interview them as they load their bags into the car.

What is striking is the wide gap between what they say they did, and what I observed. I can ask them how long they spent in-store and the answer is again different from the one on the stopwatch in my pocket. I found that consumers generally reported that time spent in-store was roughly twice that on our stopwatch. One consumer reported the in-store time as approximately one hour; our stopwatch read 28 minutes. Ask them what they bought, and often the throw-ins I saw them buy are somehow forgotten.

This holiday shopping season, those shoppers may encounter the most crowded stores ever. With temperate weather across the country, winter merchandise is still sitting on the floor. Warehouses and distribution centers are full. Manufacturers have pulled money out of print and broadcast ads and put it into in-store promotion, which might include signs and interactive displays. Department stores, in particular, crowd the aisles with promotional displays during the holidays.

Here is my advice for the industry: Emulate your customers and start to cut back. First, we have too many stores. Most chains would be healthier if they closed underperforming locations, or the lowest performing 25 percent, and studied carefully their top 25 percent successful locations. Talk to the customers. Look at what they buy in-store and online, and go into their homes and listen to them. Then test.

For consumers, my advice is this: Never shop tired, never shop hungry, and keep a list of shopping objectives. And if the deal looks too good to be true, pay attention to your instincts and just step around it. Don't buy for "someday" — if you can't wear it or use it today, chances are it will become clutter in your home instead of in the store. The best gifts for those you're unsure about are the disappearing gifts, such as flowers, chocolates, luxurious soap or wine.

Get rid of everything you don't use, love or need. Donate it, shred it, trash it. Life is too short to keep clutter around. Leave that to the stores.

PACO UNDERHILL is the chief executive of Envirosell Inc. and the author, most recently, of "What Women Want: The Science of Female Shopping."

An Ode to Shopping Malls

BY STEVEN KURUTZ | JULY 26, 2017

Farewell, pleasure palaces of days past. A filmmaker's series chronicles a way of life as it reaches its end.

ONE DAY IN 2015, Dan Bell left his home in Baltimore and drove into the suburbs to visit the Owings Mills Mall. It was a trip out of memory. As a 9-year-old boy, he had attended the grand opening of this 820,000-square-foot shopping emporium with his family.

Gold dust and pink feathers rained down from the glass-roof atrium that day as thousands gathered. Saks Fifth Avenue was an anchor tenant. The food court, lined with palm trees, was called the Conservatory. The NBC station in Baltimore dispatched its Copter Cam 2 to sweep over the parking lot and broadcast shots of the ocean of cars. Mr. Bell remembered his aunt driving around for 45 minutes to find a spot.

This was 1986, a peak mall year in America. At least one new shopping mall had been built in the United States every year since the 1950s, and 19 opened in 1990 alone. To capture the spirit of the time, Esquire dispatched a writer to the Chicago suburbs to follow two teenage boys on a typical Saturday night of mall cruising. Movies of the era, like "The Blues Brothers" (1980), "Fast Times at Ridgemont High" (1982), "True Stories" (1986), "Clueless" (1995), "Mallrats" (1995) and "Jackie Brown" (1997), included key sequences set within these "cathedrals of consumption," a term coined by the sociologist George Ritzer to describe large indoor shopping spaces.

If you were remotely involved in the booming consumer culture in those years, you spent hours circling indoor fountains and riding escalators while sucking down an Orange Julius. Even the eternally alienated Joan Didion wrote of buying two straw hats, four bottles of nail enamel and "a toaster, on sale at Sears," at the Ala Moana Center in Honolulu.

At the time of his return visit in 2015, Mr. Bell had not been to the mall in Owings Mills, Md. — or any shopping mall — in more than a decade. Although he had heard that it was struggling, he was not prepared for what he saw.

"The first moment kind of took my breath away, because it was this entire corridor of nothing," Mr. Bell said.

The French marble floors still gleamed under artificial light. It wasn't quite a ruin, but it looked as if a viral outbreak had removed all life from the place.

"They had loud pop music echoing through the mall, and I'm looking down this corridor, and there's no people, no stores open," Mr. Bell said. "It was really a sobering moment."

You can see his hushed reaction in the 10-minute video he filmed that day and posted to YouTube. Owings Mills turned out to be the pilot episode for what Mr. Bell, a 40-year-old filmmaker, has called the "Dead Mall Series" — a visual journey through the Mid-Atlantic States focused on the dying pleasure palaces of his youth.

Others have found creative grist in the dead-mall phenomenon. In her best-selling thriller "Gone Girl," Gillian Flynn set a scene in a four-story destination mall gone to seed in a Missouri suburb. What was once the beating heart of the community had become "two million square feet of echo." The author wrote the mall into the novel and kept it in her screenplay for the film adaptation, because, she said: "For kids of the '80s especially, dead malls have a very strong allure. We were the last of the free-range kids, roaming around malls, not really buying anything, but just looking. To see all those big looming spaces so empty now — it's a childhood haunting."

Narrated in a low-key voice-over and set to a downbeat soundtrack of retro-synth Vaporwave music, Mr. Bell's video shorts pay affectionate tribute to and try to understand a fallen world. They evoke the same fuzzy '80s nostalgia as the recent time-capsule photo book "Malls Across America" by Michael Galinsky, even as they offer an unsettling visual document of the retail apocalypse that changing consumer

Burlington Center Mall in Burlington, N.J.

habits, e-commerce and economic disparity have wrought. A report issued by Credit Suisse in June predicted that 20 to 25 percent of the more than 1,000 existing enclosed malls in America will close in the next five years.

Though upscale malls in wealthy communities continue to do well, Mr. Bell isn't interested in those; he visits dead malls, and among the deadest are ones in working-class and rural communities. Filming at the Bristol Mall in Bristol, Va., Mr. Bell discovered 10 stores that remained open in the entire center; the rest of the retail spaces sat empty behind lowered metal gates.

At the Rehoboth Mall in Rehoboth Beach, Del., he met a middle-aged immigrant couple running a clothing alteration business in a space that had once been the food court. Weird moments abound in the series, as when Mr. Bell's camera fixes on a forgotten corner to underscore the desolation, and then a geriatric mall-walker appears in frame, doing solitary laps.

Dan Bell, the creator of the "Dead Mall Series" on YouTube, in the Voorhees Town Center, a mall in central New Jersey.

In his running commentary, Mr. Bell is part affable tour guide ("Heading down this corridor, you can see ahead there, that's where the Sears used to be"), part mall-architecture buff ("Do I love this vintage brick planter? Yes") and part baffled Everyman ("There's no customers, but they have a customer-service desk").

Watching the "Dead Mall Series" provokes in the viewer a conflicting swirl of emotions. You think of your own happy times in malls and feel sad for the loss, and then feel stupid for getting all emotional about what was an artificial and manipulative experience built around shopping.

Malls are an emotional subject, Mr. Bell has discovered: "The things people write me are incredible. From young people who just love the retro aspect to people who experienced things in malls that are meaningful. First dates, meeting their husband or wife, their first job."

The short history of malls goes like this: In 1954, Victor Gruen's Northland Center, often credited as the first modern shopping mall (though earlier examples existed), opens in Southfield, Mich. The suburban location is fitting because the rise of the automobile, helped along by the Federal-Aid Highway Act, led to the widespread creation of large shopping centers away from urban centers. This, among other factors, nearly killed downtowns, and malls reigned supreme for some 40 years. By the 1990s, however, a new urbanism movement revived the urban shopping experience and eroded the dominance of malls. Next, the rise of big box stores and online shopping sounded the death knell for mall culture.

"People who are in the malls, who went to malls, this is the mourning period right now, because we are losing a lot of malls," Mr. Bell said. "It's hard for some people."

In the Marley Station Mall episode, filmed in January in Glen Burnie, Md., Mr. Bell related a personal story. Training his camera on a steel abstract sculpture, he says, "The shoe store was right in front of that sculpture. It's now a Spencer's, but at the time it was a Dolcis. And I worked there because my friend managed it. So I stared at that sculpture every single day from work."

Marley Station was Mr. Bell's home mall. He could get there in 15 minutes if he managed to swing a ride, an hour if he walked. Like Ms. Flynn and a whole generation of middle and lower-middle-class suburban kids, for Mr. Bell the mall was the place to go. Chess King and Regal Cinema beckoned. "You would sit outside and smoke cigarettes and walk around inside and see who's there," Mr. Bell said.

Mr. Bell's favorite store in the mall was Suncoast Motion Picture Company. He would spend half the afternoon digging through videotapes in the $10 rack and finding weird little cult films like "The Honeymoon Killers" and "Street Trash." Then he would stroll down to Walden Books and spend more happy hours in the film section.

In those years the mall was derided as an alienating place filled with soulless chain stores, but it was possible to get something of a cultural education there.

Libraries, Gardens, Museums. Oh, and a Clothing Store.

BY VANESSA FRIEDMAN | NOV. 19, 2018

Shopping areas in Asia are about the experience, not just the retail sale.

SHHH. DO YOU HEAR THAT? It's the sound of wind whistling through the abandoned malls of America as the Cassandras of contemporary retail cry their doom through corridors lined by fronds of lonely greenery: the end of a way of shopping, and all that.

But train your ears toward another direction. In Asia, an entirely different story is being sung: one full of glimmer and potential; one that is not limited to luxury products but treats all customers as if they were buying luxury; one in which consumers are drawn like magnets to the physical reality of a — what to call it? Not a bazaar, really, or an arcade, or a plaza. An immersive aesthetic experience with shopping as a byproduct, perhaps.

In Shanghai, the Shanghai Village, an outlet shopping complex created by Value Retail (founder of Bicester Village in Oxford, England) in a Disney resort area, stretches for 473,612 square feet across the waterfront, its gleaming Art Deco promenades lined by 200 trees and featuring bathroom lounges covered in swirling mosaics in the styles of different artists and so eye-popping they are actually booked for local events on their own.

In Seoul, the 30,140-square-foot library in the COEX Mall includes approximately 50,000 books and magazines to browse, and offers couches and reading tables for passers-by as well as serving as a venue for cultural events.

In Siem Reap, Cambodia, the 86,000-square-foot T Galleria by DFS (yes, the "duty free" folks, though this is not your standard airport experience) houses a multitude of brands alongside reflecting pools, verdant gardens and work from local artisans.

The T Galleria by DFS in Siem Reap, Cambodia. The almost 60-foot-long art installation hanging in the central atrium was inspired by the warm colors of Buddhist monks' robes.

And in Hong Kong, on the Kowloon side of the harbor, a $2.6 billion, three million-square-foot art and design district 10 years in the making, called Victoria Dockside, is being built by Adrian Cheng's New World Development Company. It ultimately will include an art museum, a soaring green wall, an ultraluxury hotel, apartments, offices and — of course — retail, framed like the art that surrounds it.

To name a few.

Together, these projects embody a new way of thinking about the physical space where stores congregate, one that borrows from the online playbook: prioritizing the idea of content over contents, and further demonstrating the way in which the real and virtual worlds increasingly intertwine. Not because they offer video screens or iPads for ordering (though they are on hand) but because of a more fundamental conceptual connectivity.

"It's a core reality shift," said Scott Malkin, the founder and chairman of Value Retail. "The war is over. Alibaba won. That means physical retail is no longer about the distribution of goods but building brand equity."

And brand equity is created via the subliminal communication of ephemeral values: service and touch — what Mr. Malkin calls "the software" that surrounds the "hardware" of bricks and mortar (and marble and sandstone) reality. Which then becomes the place, he said, "where the interface behavior occurs."

"The context for stores is more and more important," said Luca Solca, head of luxury goods research at Exane BNP Paribas, "because you have to make people want to get out of their homes and away from their screens.

"It's not just about the store itself," he added. "It's retail counter-standardization."

If the old model — the merch emporium — gave way during the turn of the millennium to the flagship model, which saw stores become echoing and somewhat austere temples where consumers worshiped the handbag on the plinth, we are now entering a new stage. One embodied more by Apple or Starbucks than any previous fashion retail space.

One that takes the rising principles of the experience economy and the growing belief that millennial consumers — who hate anything smacking of marketing or overt product pushing — are increasingly choosing to spend their money on the unique event rather than on the aspirational product, and applies them to shopping.

One that says investing in a value system that surrounds the shopping experience will pay off in consumption. Because instead of taking home a postcard or a T-shirt to remember the visit, you take home a Prada shoe, or a Dior dress.

Mr. Cheng first began exploring these principles in 2009 in his K-11 Art Mall developments in Hong Kong, Shanghai and Guangzhou, which originally combined art and shopping elements — a mix of high and consumer culture previously seen as heretical — and then expanded from there. The Shanghai Art Mall, for example, includes an urban farm where visitors can grow herbs that they eventually take home for their dinner. It's not an obvious sales driver but, Mr. Cheng said on stage at The New York Times International Luxury conference in Hong Kong last week, foot traffic went up dramatically after it was opened.

Not that the point was "about traffic," Mr. Cheng said. "It's about building a community. About grooming the audience and having access to their behavior, which then continues online." The farm is the bait, in a sense.

Going to a store, Mr. Malkin said, "should feel like going to a hotel or resort, where you are taking away a memory because you are touched by an emotion you want to revisit." As a retailer, this means "you are not serving a person who needs an item," he said. "You are serving a person who needs an experience." And that changes how the retailer does things.

Mr. Solca said he believed this kind of strategic approach would form a new model for global retail. Mr. Malkin agrees.

"The reality is our experience in China will set the gold standard for what's possible in other international locations," he said. "It's driving our thinking about the future."

Just whatever you do, don't call it a "shopping center."

VANESSA FRIEDMAN is The Times's fashion director and chief fashion critic. She was previously the fashion editor of the Financial Times.

CHAPTER 2

Targeting Consumers

Most consumers think of their purchases as individual choices, fulfilling specific needs or desires. What they may not realize is that their decisions are constantly scrutinized and studied by sellers in order to better understand why consumers buy what they buy. And, in fact, some purchasing decisions may not be as autonomous as they might seem. In this chapter, the articles examine the means and methods by which companies target their consumers and make sense of their consumption patterns.

How Companies Learn Your Secrets

BY CHARLES DUHIGG | FEB. 16, 2012

ANDREW POLE HAD just started working as a statistician for Target in 2002, when two colleagues from the marketing department stopped by his desk to ask an odd question: "If we wanted to figure out if a customer is pregnant, even if she didn't want us to know, can you do that?"

Pole has a master's degree in statistics and another in economics, and has been obsessed with the intersection of data and human behavior most of his life. His parents were teachers in North Dakota, and while other kids were going to 4-H, Pole was doing algebra and writing computer programs. "The stereotype of a math nerd is true," he told me when I spoke with him last year. "I kind of like going out and evangelizing analytics."

As the marketers explained to Pole — and as Pole later explained to me, back when we were still speaking and before Target told him to stop — new parents are a retailer's holy grail. Most shoppers don't buy everything they need at one store. Instead, they buy groceries at the grocery store and toys at the toy store, and they visit Target only when they need certain items they associate with Target — cleaning supplies, say, or new socks or a six-month supply of toilet paper. But Target sells everything from milk to stuffed animals to lawn furniture to electronics, so one of the company's primary goals is convincing customers that the only store they need is Target. But it's a tough message to get across, even with the most ingenious ad campaigns, because once consumers' shopping habits are ingrained, it's incredibly difficult to change them.

There are, however, some brief periods in a person's life when old routines fall apart and buying habits are suddenly in flux. One of those moments — *the* moment, really — is right around the birth of a child, when parents are exhausted and overwhelmed and their shopping patterns and brand loyalties are up for grabs. But as Target's marketers explained to Pole, timing is everything. Because birth records are usually public, the moment a couple have a new baby, they are almost instantaneously barraged with offers and incentives and advertisements from all sorts of companies. Which means that the key is to reach them earlier, before any other retailers know a baby is on the way. Specifically, the marketers said they wanted to send specially designed ads to women in their second trimester, which is when most expectant mothers begin buying all sorts of new things, like prenatal vitamins and maternity clothing. "Can you give us a list?" the marketers asked.

"We knew that if we could identify them in their second trimester, there's a good chance we could capture them for years," Pole told me. "As soon as we get them buying diapers from us, they're going to start buying everything else too. If you're rushing through the store, looking for bottles, and you pass orange juice, you'll grab a carton. Oh, and there's that new DVD I want. Soon, you'll be buying cereal and paper towels from us, and keep coming back."

The desire to collect information on customers is not new for Target or any other large retailer, of course. For decades, Target has collected vast amounts of data on every person who regularly walks into one of its stores. Whenever possible, Target assigns each shopper a unique code — known internally as the Guest ID number — that keeps tabs on everything they buy. "If you use a credit card or a coupon, or fill out a survey, or mail in a refund, or call the customer help line, or open an e-mail we've sent you or visit our Web site, we'll record it and link it to your Guest ID," Pole said. "We want to know everything we can."

Also linked to your Guest ID is demographic information like your age, whether you are married and have kids, which part of town you live in, how long it takes you to drive to the store, your estimated salary, whether you've moved recently, what credit cards you carry in your wallet and what Web sites you visit. Target can buy data about your ethnicity, job history, the magazines you read, if you've ever declared bankruptcy or got divorced, the year you bought (or lost) your house, where you went to college, what kinds of topics you talk about online, whether you prefer certain brands of coffee, paper towels, cereal or applesauce, your political leanings, reading habits, charitable giving and the number of cars you own. (In a statement, Target declined to identify what demographic information it collects or purchases.) All that information is meaningless, however, without someone to analyze and make sense of it. That's where Andrew Pole and the dozens of other members of Target's Guest Marketing Analytics department come in.

Almost every major retailer, from grocery chains to investmentbanks to the U.S. Postal Service, has a "predictive analytics" department devoted to understanding not just consumers' shopping habits but also their personal habits, so as to more efficiently market to them. "But Target has always been one of the smartest at this," says Eric Siegel, a consultant and the chairman of a conference called Predictive Analytics World. "We're living through a golden age of behavioral research. It's amazing how much we can figure out about how people think now."

The reason Target can snoop on our shopping habits is that, over the past two decades, the science of habit formation has become a major field of research in neurology and psychology departments at hundreds of major medical centers and universities, as well as inside extremely well financed corporate labs. "It's like an arms race to hire statisticians nowadays," said Andreas Weigend, the former chief scientist at Amazon.com. "Mathematicians are suddenly sexy." As the ability to analyze data has grown more and more fine-grained, the push to understand how daily habits influence our decisions has become one of the most exciting topics in clinical research, even though most of us are hardly aware those patterns exist. One study from Duke University estimated that habits, rather than conscious decision-making, shape 45 percent of the choices we make every day, and recent discoveries have begun to change everything from the way we think about dieting to how doctors conceive treatments for anxiety, depression and addictions.

This research is also transforming our understanding of how habits function across organizations and societies. A football coach named Tony Dungy propelled one of the worst teams in the N.F.L. to the Super Bowl by focusing on how his players habitually reacted to on-field cues. Before he became Treasury secretary, Paul O'Neill overhauled a stumbling conglomerate, Alcoa, and turned it into a top performer in the Dow Jones by relentlessly attacking one habit — a specific approach to worker safety — which in turn caused a companywide transformation. The Obama campaign has hired a habit specialist as its "chief scientist" to figure out how to trigger new voting patterns among different constituencies.

Researchers have figured out how to stop people from habitually overeating and biting their nails. They can explain why some of us automatically go for a jog every morning and are more productive at work, while others oversleep and procrastinate. There is a calculus, it turns out, for mastering our subconscious urges. For companies like Target, the exhaustive rendering of our conscious and unconscious patterns into data sets and algorithms has revolutionized what they know about us and, therefore, how precisely they can sell.

Inside the brain-and-cognitive-sciences department of the Massachusetts Institute of Technology are what, to the casual observer, look like dollhouse versions of surgical theaters. There are rooms with tiny scalpels, small drills and miniature saws. Even the operating tables are petite, as if prepared for 7-year-old surgeons. Inside those shrunken O.R.'s, neurologists cut into the skulls of anesthetized rats, implanting tiny sensors that record the smallest changes in the activity of their brains.

An M.I.T. neuroscientist named Ann Graybiel told me that she and her colleagues began exploring habits more than a decade ago by putting their wired rats into a T-shaped maze with chocolate at one end. The maze was structured so that each animal was positioned behind a barrier that opened after a loud click. The first time a rat was placed in the maze, it would usually wander slowly up and down the center aisle after the barrier slid away, sniffing in corners and scratching at walls. It appeared to smell the chocolate but couldn't figure out how to find it. There was no discernible pattern in the rat's meanderings and no indication it was working hard to find the treat.

The probes in the rats' heads, however, told a different story. While each animal wandered through the maze, its brain was working furiously. Every time a rat sniffed the air or scratched a wall, the neurosensors inside the animal's head exploded with activity. As the scientists repeated the experiment, again and again, the rats eventually stopped sniffing corners and making wrong turns and began to zip through the maze with more and more speed. And within their brains, something unexpected occurred: as each rat learned how to complete the maze more quickly, its mental activity *decreased*. As the path became more and more automatic — as it became a habit — the rats started thinking less and less.

This process, in which the brain converts a sequence of actions into an automatic routine, is called "chunking." There are dozens, if not hundreds, of behavioral chunks we rely on every day. Some are simple: you automatically put toothpaste on your toothbrush before sticking it in your mouth. Some, like making the kids' lunch, are a little more complex. Still others are so complicated that it's remarkable to realize that a habit could have emerged at all.

Take backing your car out of the driveway. When you first learned to drive, that act required a major dose of concentration, and for good reason: it involves peering into the rearview and side mirrors and checking for obstacles, putting your foot on the brake, moving the gearshift into reverse, removing your foot from the brake, estimating the distance between the garage and the street while keeping the wheels aligned, calculating how images in the mirrors translate into actual distances, all while applying differing amounts of pressure to the gas pedal and brake.

Now, you perform that series of actions every time you pull into the street without thinking very much. Your brain has chunked large parts of it. Left to its own devices, the brain will try to make almost any repeated behavior into a habit, because habits allow our minds to conserve effort. But conserving mental energy is tricky, because if our brains power down at the wrong moment, we might fail to notice something important, like a child riding her bike down the sidewalk or a speeding car coming down the street. So we've devised a clever system to determine when to let a habit take over. It's something that happens whenever a chunk of behavior starts or ends — and it helps to explain why habits are so difficult to change once they're formed, despite our best intentions.

To understand this a little more clearly, consider again the chocolate-seeking rats. What Graybiel and her colleagues found was that, as the ability to navigate the maze became habitual, there were two spikes in the rats' brain activity — once at the beginning of the maze, when the rat heard the click right before the barrier slid away, and once at the end, when the rat found the chocolate. Those spikes show when the rats' brains were fully engaged, and the dip in neural activity between the spikes showed when the habit took over. From behind the partition, the rat wasn't sure what waited on the other side, until it heard the click, which it had come to associate with the maze. Once it heard that sound, it knew to use the "maze habit," and its brain activity decreased. Then at the end of the routine, when the reward appeared, the brain shook itself awake again and the chocolate signaled to the rat that this particular habit was worth remembering, and the neurological pathway was carved that much deeper.

The process within our brains that creates habits is a three-step loop. First, there is a cue, a trigger that tells your brain to go into automatic mode and which habit to use. Then there is the routine, which can be physical or mental or emotional. Finally, there is a reward, which helps your brain figure out if this particular loop is worth remembering for the future. Over time, this loop — cue, routine, reward; cue, routine, reward — becomes more and more automatic. The cue and reward become neurologically intertwined until a sense of craving emerges. What's unique about cues and rewards, however, is how subtle they can be. Neurological studies like the ones in Graybiel's lab have revealed that some cues span just milliseconds. And rewards can range from the obvious (like the sugar rush that a morning doughnut habit provides) to the infinitesimal (like the barely noticeable — but measurable — sense of relief the brain experiences after successfully navigating the driveway). Most cues and rewards, in fact, happen so quickly and are so slight that we are hardly aware of them at all. But our neural systems notice and use them to build automatic behaviors.

Habits aren't destiny — they can be ignored, changed or replaced. But it's also true that once the loop is established and a habit emerges, your brain stops fully participating in decision-making. So unless you deliberately fight a habit — unless you find new cues and rewards — the old pattern will unfold automatically.

"We've done experiments where we trained rats to run down a maze until it was a habit, and then we extinguished the habit by changing the placement of the reward," Graybiel told me. "Then one day, we'll put the reward in the old place and put in the rat and, by golly, the old habit will re-emerge right away. Habits never really disappear."

Luckily, simply understanding how habits work makes them easier to control. Take, for instance, a series of studies conducted a few years ago at Columbia University and the University of Alberta. Researchers wanted to understand how exercise habits emerge. In one project, 256 members of a health-insurance plan were invited to classes stressing the importance of exercise. Half the participants received an extra lesson on the theories of habit formation (the structure of the habit loop) and were asked to identify cues and rewards that might help them develop exercise routines.

The results were dramatic. Over the next four months, those participants who deliberately identified cues and rewards spent twice as much time exercising as their peers. Other studies have yielded similar results. According to another recent paper, if you want to start running in the morning, it's essential that you choose a simple cue (like always putting on your sneakers before breakfast or leaving your running clothes next to your bed) and a clear reward (like a midday treat or even the sense of accomplishment that comes from ritually recording your miles in a log book). After a while, your brain will start anticipating that reward — craving the treat or the feeling of accomplishment — and there will be a measurable neurological impulse to lace up your jogging shoes each morning.

Our relationship to e-mail operates on the same principle. When a computer chimes or a smartphone vibrates with a new message, the brain starts anticipating the neurological "pleasure" (even if we don't recognize it as such) that clicking on the e-mail and reading it provides. That expectation, if unsatisfied, can build until you find yourself moved to distraction by the thought of an e-mail sitting there unread — even if you know, rationally, it's most likely not important. On the other hand, once you remove the cue by disabling the buzzing of your phone or the chiming of your computer, the craving is never triggered, and you'll find, over time, that you're able to work productively for long stretches without checking your in-box.

Some of the most ambitious habit experiments have been conducted by corporate America. To understand why executives are so entranced by this science, consider how one of the world's largest companies, Procter & Gamble, used habit insights to turn a failing product into one of its biggest sellers. P. & G. is the corporate behemoth behind a whole range of products, from Downy fabric softener to Bounty paper towels to Duracell batteries and dozens of other household brands. In the mid-1990s, P. & G.'s executives began a secret project to create a new product that could eradicate bad smells. P. & G. spent millions developing a colorless, cheap-to-manufacture liquid that could be sprayed on a smoky blouse, stinky couch, old jacket or stained car interior and make it odorless. In order to market the product — Febreze — the company formed a team that included a former Wall Street mathematician named Drake Stimson and habit specialists, whose job was to make sure the television commercials, which they tested in Phoenix, Salt Lake City and Boise, Idaho, accentuated the product's cues and rewards just right.

The first ad showed a woman complaining about the smoking section of a restaurant. Whenever she eats there, she says, her jacket smells like smoke. A friend tells her that if she uses Febreze, it will eliminate the odor. The cue in the ad is clear: the harsh smell of cigarette smoke. The reward: odor eliminated from clothes. The second ad featured a woman worrying about her dog, Sophie, who always sits on the couch. "Sophie will always smell like Sophie," she says, but with Febreze, "now my furniture doesn't have to." The ads were put in heavy rotation. Then the marketers sat back, anticipating how they would spend their bonuses. A week passed. Then two. A month. Two months. Sales started small and got smaller. Febreze was a dud.

The panicked marketing team canvassed consumers and conducted in-depth interviews to figure out what was going wrong,

Stimson recalled. Their first inkling came when they visited a woman's home outside Phoenix. The house was clean and organized. She was something of a neat freak, the woman explained. But when P. & G.'s scientists walked into her living room, where her nine cats spent most of their time, the scent was so overpowering that one of them gagged.

According to Stimson, who led the Febreze team, a researcher asked the woman, "What do you do about the cat smell?"

"It's usually not a problem," she said.

"Do you smell it now?"

"No," she said. "Isn't it wonderful? They hardly smell at all!"

A similar scene played out in dozens of other smelly homes. The reason Febreze wasn't selling, the marketers realized, was that people couldn't detect most of the bad smells in their lives. If you live with nine cats, you become desensitized to their scents. If you smoke cigarettes, eventually you don't smell smoke anymore. Even the strongest odors fade with constant exposure. That's why Febreze was a failure. The product's cue — the bad smells that were supposed to trigger daily use — was hidden from the people who needed it the most. And Febreze's reward (an odorless home) was meaningless to someone who couldn't smell offensive scents in the first place.

P. & G. employed a Harvard Business School professor to analyze Febreze's ad campaigns. They collected hours of footage of people cleaning their homes and watched tape after tape, looking for clues that might help them connect Febreze to people's daily habits. When that didn't reveal anything, they went into the field and conducted more interviews. A breakthrough came when they visited a woman in a suburb near Scottsdale, Ariz., who was in her 40s with four children. Her house was clean, though not compulsively tidy, and didn't appear to have any odor problems; there were no pets or smokers. To the surprise of everyone, she loved Febreze.

"I use it every day," she said.

"What smells are you trying to get rid of?" a researcher asked.

"I don't really use it for specific smells," the woman said. "I use it for normal cleaning — a couple of sprays when I'm done in a room."

The researchers followed her around as she tidied the house. In the bedroom, she made her bed, tightened the sheet's corners, then sprayed the comforter with Febreze. In the living room, she vacuumed, picked up the children's shoes, straightened the coffee table, then sprayed Febreze on the freshly cleaned carpet.

"It's nice, you know?" she said. "Spraying feels like a little minicelebration when I'm done with a room." At the rate she was going, the team estimated, she would empty a bottle of Febreze every two weeks.

When they got back to P. & G.'s headquarters, the researchers watched their videotapes again. Now they knew what to look for and saw their mistake in scene after scene. Cleaning has its own habit loops that already exist. In one video, when a woman walked into a dirty room (cue), she started sweeping and picking up toys (routine), then she examined the room and smiled when she was done (reward). In another, a woman scowled at her unmade bed (cue), proceeded to straighten the blankets and comforter (routine) and then sighed as she ran her hands over the freshly plumped pillows (reward). P. & G. had been trying to create a whole new habit with Febreze, but what they really needed to do was piggyback on habit loops that were already in place. The marketers needed to position Febreze as something that came at the end of the cleaning ritual, the reward, rather than as a whole new cleaning routine.

The company printed new ads showing open windows and gusts of fresh air. More perfume was added to the Febreze formula, so that instead of merely neutralizing odors, the spray had its own distinct scent. Television commercials were filmed of women, having finished their cleaning routine, using Febreze to spritz freshly made beds and just-laundered clothing. Each ad was designed to appeal to the habit loop: when you see a freshly cleaned room (cue), pull out Febreze (routine) and enjoy a smell that says you've done a great job (reward). When you finish making a bed (cue), spritz Febreze (routine) and breathe a sweet, contented sigh (reward). Febreze, the ads implied, was a pleasant treat, not a reminder that your home stinks.

And so Febreze, a product originally conceived as a revolutionary way to destroy odors, became an air freshener used once things are already clean. The Febreze revamp occurred in the summer of 1998. Within two months, sales doubled. A year later, the product brought in $230 million. Since then Febreze has spawned dozens of spinoffs — air fresheners, candles and laundry detergents — that now account for sales of more than $1 billion a year. Eventually, P. & G. began mentioning to customers that, in addition to smelling sweet, Febreze can actually kill bad odors. Today it's one of the top-selling products in the world.

Andrew Pole was hired by Target to use the same kinds of insights into consumers' habits to expand Target's sales. His assignment was to analyze all the cue-routine-reward loops among shoppers and help the company figure out how to exploit them. Much of his department's work was straightforward: find the customers who have children and send them catalogs that feature toys before Christmas. Look for shoppers who habitually purchase swimsuits in April and send them coupons for sunscreen in July and diet books in December. But Pole's most important assignment was to identify those unique moments in consumers' lives when their shopping habits become particularly flexible and the right advertisement or coupon would cause them to begin spending in new ways.

In the 1980s, a team of researchers led by a U.C.L.A. professor named Alan Andreasen undertook a study of peoples' most mundane purchases, like soap, toothpaste, trash bags and toilet paper. They learned that most shoppers paid almost no attention to how they bought these products, that the purchases occurred habitually, without any complex decision-making. Which meant it was hard for marketers, despite their displays and coupons and product promotions, to persuade shoppers to change.

But when some customers were going through a major life event, like graduating from college or getting a new job or moving to a new town, their shopping habits became flexible in ways that were both predictable and potential gold mines for retailers. The study found that when someone marries, he or she is more likely to start buying a new type of coffee. When a couple move into a new house, they're more apt to purchase a different kind of cereal. When they divorce, there's an increased chance they'll start buying different brands of beer.

Consumers going through major life events often don't notice, or care, that their shopping habits have shifted, but retailers notice, and they care quite a bit. At those unique moments, Andreasen wrote, customers are "vulnerable to intervention by marketers." In other words, a precisely timed advertisement, sent to a recent divorcee or new homebuyer, can change someone's shopping patterns for years.

And among life events, none are more important than the arrival of a baby. At that moment, new parents' habits are more flexible than at almost any other time in their adult lives. If companies can identify pregnant shoppers, they can earn millions.

The only problem is that identifying pregnant customers is harder than it sounds. Target has a baby-shower registry, and Pole started there, observing how shopping habits changed as a woman approached her due date, which women on the registry had willingly disclosed. He ran test after test, analyzing the data, and before long some useful patterns emerged. Lotions, for example. Lots of people buy lotion, but one of Pole's colleagues noticed that women on the baby registry were buying larger quantities of unscented lotion around the beginning of their second trimester. Another analyst noted that sometime in the first 20 weeks, pregnant women loaded up on supplements like calcium, magnesium and zinc. Many shoppers purchase soap and cotton balls, but when someone suddenly starts buying lots of scent-free soap and extra-big bags of cotton balls, in addition to hand sanitizers and washcloths, it signals they could be getting close to their delivery date.

As Pole's computers crawled through the data, he was able to identify about 25 products that, when analyzed together, allowed him to assign each shopper a "pregnancy prediction" score. More important, he could also estimate her due date to within a small window, so Target could send coupons timed to very specific stages of her pregnancy.

One Target employee I spoke to provided a hypothetical example. Take a fictional Target shopper named Jenny Ward, who is 23, lives in Atlanta and in March bought cocoa-butter lotion, a purse large enough to double as a diaper bag, zinc and magnesium supplements and a bright blue rug. There's, say, an 87 percent chance that she's pregnant and that her delivery date is sometime in late August. What's more, because of the data attached to her Guest ID number, Target knows how to trigger Jenny's habits. They know that if she receives a coupon via e-mail, it will most likely cue her to buy online. They know that if she receives an ad in the mail on Friday, she frequently uses it on a weekend trip to the store. And they know that if they reward her with a printed receipt that entitles her to a free cup of Starbucks coffee, she'll use it when she comes back again.

In the past, that knowledge had limited value. After all, Jenny purchased only cleaning supplies at Target, and there were only so many psychological buttons the company could push. But now that she is pregnant, everything is up for grabs. In addition to triggering Jenny's habits to buy more cleaning products, they can also start including offers for an array of products, some more obvious than others, that a woman at her stage of pregnancy might need.

Pole applied his program to every regular female shopper in Target's national database and soon had a list of tens of thousands of women who were most likely pregnant. If they could entice those women or their husbands to visit Target and buy baby-related products, the company's cue-routine-reward calculators could kick in and start pushing them to buy groceries, bathing suits, toys and clothing, as well. When Pole shared his list with the marketers, he said, they were ecstatic. Soon, Pole was getting invited to meetings above his paygrade. Eventually his paygrade went up.

At which point someone asked an important question: How are women going to react when they figure out how much Target knows?

"If we send someone a catalog and say, 'Congratulations on your first child!' and they've never told us they're pregnant, that's going to make some people uncomfortable," Pole told me. "We are very conservative about compliance with all privacy laws. But even if you're following the law, you can do things where people get queasy."

About a year after Pole created his pregnancy-prediction model, a man walked into a Target outside Minneapolis and demanded to see the manager. He was clutching coupons that had been sent to his daughter, and he was angry, according to an employee who participated in the conversation.

"My daughter got this in the mail!" he said. "She's still in high school, and you're sending her coupons for baby clothes and cribs? Are you trying to encourage her to get pregnant?"

The manager didn't have any idea what the man was talking about. He looked at the mailer. Sure enough, it was addressed to the man's daughter and contained advertisements for maternity clothing, nursery furniture and pictures of smiling infants. The manager apologized and then called a few days later to apologize again.

On the phone, though, the father was somewhat abashed. "I had a talk with my daughter," he said. "It turns out there's been some activities in my house I haven't been completely aware of. She's due in August. I owe you an apology."

When I approached Target to discuss Pole's work, its representatives declined to speak with me. "Our mission is to make Target the preferred shopping destination for our guests by delivering outstanding value, continuous innovation and exceptional guest experience," the company wrote in a statement. "We've developed a number of research tools that allow us to gain insights into trends and preferences within different demographic segments of our guest population." When I sent Target a complete summary of my reporting, the reply was more terse: "Almost all of your statements contain inaccurate information and publishing them would be misleading to the public. We do not intend to address each statement point by point." The company declined to identify what was inaccurate. They did add, however, that Target "is in compliance with all federal and state laws, including those related to protected health information."

When I offered to fly to Target's headquarters to discuss its concerns, a spokeswoman e-mailed that no one would meet me. When I flew out anyway, I was told I was on a list of prohibited visitors. "I've been instructed not to give you access and to ask you to leave," said a very nice security guard named Alex.

Using data to predict a woman's pregnancy, Target realized soon after Pole perfected his model, could be a public-relations disaster. So the question became: how could they get their advertisements into expectant mothers' hands without making it appear they were spying on them? How do you take advantage of someone's habits without letting them know you're studying their lives?

Before I met Andrew Pole, before I even decided to write a book about the science of habit formation, I had another goal: I wanted to lose weight.

I had got into a bad habit of going to the cafeteria every afternoon and eating a chocolate-chip cookie, which contributed to my gaining a few pounds. Eight, to be precise. I put a Post-it note on my computer reading "NO MORE COOKIES." But every afternoon, I managed to ignore that note, wander to the cafeteria, buy a cookie and eat it while chatting with colleagues. Tomorrow, I always promised myself, I'll muster the willpower to resist.

Tomorrow, I ate another cookie.

When I started interviewing experts in habit formation, I concluded each interview by asking what I should do. The first step, they said, was to figure out my habit loop. The routine was simple: every afternoon, I walked to the cafeteria, bought a cookie and ate it while chatting with friends.

Next came some less obvious questions: What was the cue? Hunger? Boredom? Low blood sugar? And what was the reward? The taste of the cookie itself? The temporary distraction from my work? The chance to socialize with colleagues?

Rewards are powerful because they satisfy cravings, but we're often not conscious of the urges driving our habits in the first place. So one day, when I felt a cookie impulse, I went outside and took a walk instead. The next day, I went to the cafeteria and bought a coffee. The next, I bought an apple and ate it while chatting with friends. You get the idea. I wanted to test different theories regarding what reward I was really craving. Was it hunger? (In which case the apple should have worked.) Was it the desire for a quick burst of energy? (If so, the coffee should suffice.) Or, as turned out to be the answer, was it that after several hours spent focused on work, I wanted to socialize, to make sure I was up to speed on office gossip, and the cookie was just a convenient excuse? When I walked to a colleague's desk and chatted for a few minutes, it turned out, my cookie urge was gone.

All that was left was identifying the cue.

Deciphering cues is hard, however. Our lives often contain too much information to figure out what is triggering a particular behavior. Do you eat breakfast at a certain time because you're hungry? Or because the morning news is on? Or because your kids have started eating? Experiments have shown that most cues fit into one of five categories: location, time, emotional state, other people or the immediately preceding action. So to figure out the cue for my cookie habit, I wrote down five things the moment the urge hit:

Where are you? (Sitting at my desk.)

What time is it? (3:36 p.m.)

What's your emotional state? (Bored.)

Who else is around? (No one.)

What action preceded the urge? (Answered an e-mail.)

The next day I did the same thing. And the next. Pretty soon, the cue was clear: I always felt an urge to snack around 3:30.

Once I figured out all the parts of the loop, it seemed fairly easy to change my habit. But the psychologists and neuroscientists warned me that, for my new behavior to stick, I needed to abide by the same principle that guided Procter & Gamble in selling Febreze: To shift the routine — to socialize, rather than eat a cookie — I needed to piggyback on an existing habit. So now, every day around 3:30, I stand up, look around the newsroom for someone to talk to, spend 10 minutes gossiping, then go back to my desk. The cue and reward have stayed the same. Only the routine has shifted. It doesn't feel like a decision, any more than the M.I.T. rats made a decision to run through the maze. It's now a habit. I've lost 21 pounds since then (12 of them from changing my cookie ritual).

After Andrew Pole built his pregnancy-prediction model, after he identified thousands of female shoppers who were most likely pregnant, after someone pointed out that some of those women might be a little upset if they received an advertisement making it obvious Target was studying their reproductive status, everyone decided to slow things down.

The marketing department conducted a few tests by choosing a small, random sample of women from Pole's list and mailing them combinations of advertisements to see how they reacted.

"We have the capacity to send every customer an ad booklet, specifically designed for them, that says, 'Here's everything you bought last week and a coupon for it,' " one Target executive told me. "We do that for grocery products all the time." But for pregnant women, Target's goal was selling them baby items they didn't even know they needed yet.

"With the pregnancy products, though, we learned that some women react badly," the executive said. "Then we started mixing in all these ads for things we knew pregnant women would never buy, so the baby ads looked random. We'd put an ad for a lawn mower next to diapers. We'd put a coupon for wineglasses next to infant clothes. That way, it looked like all the products were chosen by chance.

"And we found out that as long as a pregnant woman thinks she hasn't been spied on, she'll use the coupons. She just assumes that everyone else on her block got the same mailer for diapers and cribs. As long as we don't spook her, it works."

In other words, if Target piggybacked on existing habits — the same cues and rewards they already knew got customers to buy cleaning supplies or socks — then they could insert a new routine: buying baby products, as well. There's a cue ("Oh, a coupon for something I need!") a routine ("Buy! Buy! Buy!") and a reward ("I can take that off my list"). And once the shopper is inside the store, Target will hit her with cues and rewards to entice her to purchase everything she normally buys somewhere else. As long as Target camouflaged how much it knew, as long as the habit felt familiar, the new behavior took hold.

Soon after the new ad campaign began, Target's Mom and Baby sales exploded. The company doesn't break out figures for specific divisions, but between 2002 — when Pole was hired — and 2010, Target's revenues grew from $44 billion to $67 billion. In 2005, the company's president, Gregg Steinhafel, boasted to a room of investors about the company's "heightened focus on items and categories that appeal to specific guest segments such as mom and baby."

Pole was promoted. He has been invited to speak at conferences. "I never expected this would become such a big deal," he told me the last time we spoke.

A few weeks before this article went to press, I flew to Minneapolis to try and speak to Andrew Pole one last time. I hadn't talked to him in more than a year. Back when we were still friendly, I mentioned that my wife was seven months pregnant. We shop at Target, I told him, and had given the company our address so we could start receiving coupons in the mail. As my wife's pregnancy progressed, I noticed a subtle upswing in the number of advertisements for diapers and baby clothes arriving at our house. Pole didn't answer my e-mails or phone calls when I visited Minneapolis. I drove to his large home in a nice suburb, but no one answered the door. On my way back to the hotel, I stopped at a Target to pick up some deodorant, then also bought some T-shirts and a fancy hair gel. On a whim, I threw in some pacifiers, to see how the computers would react. Besides, our baby is now 9 months old. You can't have too many pacifiers.

When I paid, I didn't receive any sudden deals on diapers or formula, to my slight disappointment. It made sense, though: I was shopping in a city I never previously visited, at 9:45 p.m. on a weeknight, buying a random assortment of items. I was using a corporate credit card, and besides the pacifiers, hadn't purchased any of the things that a parent needs. It was clear to Target's computers that I was on a business trip. Pole's prediction calculator took one look at me, ran the numbers and decided to bide its time. Back home, the offers would eventually come. As Pole told me the last time we spoke: "Just wait. We'll be sending you coupons for things you want before you even know you want them."

CHARLES DUHIGG is a staff writer for The Times and author of "The Power of Habit: Why We Do What We Do in Life and Business," which will be published on Feb. 28.

Your Online Attention, Bought in an Instant

BY NATASHA SINGER | NOV. 17, 2012

YOU CAN BE SOLD in seconds.

No, wait: make that milliseconds.

The odds are that access to you — or at least the online you — is being bought and sold in less than the blink of an eye. On the Web, powerful algorithms are sizing you up, based on myriad data points: what you Google, the sites you visit, the ads you click. Then, in real time, the chance to show you an ad is auctioned to the highest bidder.

Not that you'd know it. These days in the hyperkinetic world of digital advertising, all of this happens automatically, and imperceptibly, to most consumers.

Ever wonder why that same ad for a car or a couch keeps popping up on your screen? Nearly always, the answer is real-time bidding, an electronic trading system that sells ad space on the Web pages people visit at the very moment they are visiting them. Think of these systems as a sort of Nasdaq stock market, only trading in audiences for online ads. Millions of bids flood in every second. And those bids — essentially what your eyeballs are worth to advertisers — could determine whether you see an ad for, say, a new Lexus or a used Ford, for sneakers or a popcorn maker.

One big player in this space is the Rubicon Project. Never heard of it? Consider this: Rubicon, based in Los Angeles, has actually eclipsed Google in one crucial area — the percentage of Internet users in the United States reached by display ads sold through its platform, according to comScore, a digital analytics company.

Rubicon is among a handful of technology companies that have quietly developed automated ad sales systems for Web site operators. The bidders are marketers seeking to identify their best prospects and pitch them before they move to the next Web page. It is a form of high-frequency trading — that souped-up business of algorithm-loving Wall Streeters. But in this case, the prize is the attention of ordinary people. And it all depends on data-mining to instantly evaluate the audiences available to see those online display ads, the ones that appear on Web sites next to or around content.

In industry parlance, each digital ad space is an impression. The value of an impression depends on several factors, like the size of the ad, the type of person who is available to see it and that person's location.

"The first impression seen by a high-value person on the opening page of a major newspaper first thing in the morning has a different value than a user from China who is 12 and has been on the Web all day long playing games," says Frank Addante, the founder and chief executive of Rubicon.

Yet for most of us, real-time bidding is invisible. About 97 percent of American Internet users interact with Rubicon's system every month, Mr. Addante says, and most of them aren't aware of it.

That worries some federal regulators and consumer advocates, who say that such electronic trading systems could unfairly stratify consumers, covertly offering better pricing to certain people while relegating others to inferior treatment. A computer-generated class system is one risk, they say, of an ad-driven Internet powered by surveillance.

"As you profile more and more people, you'll start to segregate people into 'the people you can get money out of' and 'the people you can't get money out of,' " says Dan Auerbach, a staff technologist at the Electronic Frontier Foundation, a digital civil rights group in San Francisco, who formerly worked in digital ad data-mining. "That is one of the dangers we should be worried about."

Of course, ad agencies and brands can tailor ads to Web users without real-time bidding. They can also buy ads without aiming them at narrow audience groups. But for marketers, the marriage of ad- and audience-buying is one of the benefits of real-time bidding.

Not so long ago, they simply bought ad spaces based on a site's general demographics and then showed every visitor the same ad, a practice called "spray and pray." Now marketers can aim just at their ideal customers — like football fans who earn more than $100,000 a year, or mothers in Denver in the market for an S.U.V. — showing them tailored ads at the exact moment they are available on a specific Web page.

"We are not buying content as a proxy for audience," says Paul Alfieri, the vice president for marketing at Turn, a data management company and automated buy-side platform for marketers based in Redwood City, Calif. "We are just buying who the audience is."

Still, for many consumer advocates, real-time bidding resembles nothing so much as a cattle auction.

"Online consumers are being bought and sold like chattel," says Jeffrey Chester, the executive director of the Center for Digital Democracy, a consumer group in Washington that has filed a complaint about real-time bidding with the Federal Trade Commission. "It's dehumanizing."

Frank Addante is 36 years old and given to wearing black shirts with a white Rubicon logo on the front. Rubicon is the fifth company he has started or helped to found.

In 1996, in his dorm room at the Illinois Institute of Technology, he developed and introduced a search engine. He later helped found L90, a digital ad technology company that went public and was later acquired by DoubleClick. His fourth enterprise, StrongMail Systems, provides e-mail delivery infrastructure to large companies.

While working in ad technology, Mr. Addante says, he became puzzled by the manual ad sales processes that many Web sites were using. Just a few years ago, he recalled, many sites still executed their online ad deals through the cumbersome back-and-forth of meetings, phone calls, e-mails and even faxes. The fragmented market made it hard for ad agencies and brands.

"That market was very inefficient," Mr. Addante said in an interview in Rubicon's Manhattan office, "much like the early days of manual stock trading."

Of course, other major industries already had automated sales systems. Concert arenas sold seats through Ticketmaster. Airlines sold tickets through a system called Sabre. Hotels offered rooms through Expedia.

So, in 2007, Mr. Addante and three other executives with whom he worked at L90, started Rubicon with the aim of creating an automated marketplace for Web sites to sell their ad inventory. Years earlier, Google invented a similar automated system for search ads.

"Google was the first to automate the buying and selling of search ads," Mr. Addante says. "We thought, 'why couldn't we do this with display ads, mobile and video?' "

Although real-time bidding accounts for a small portion of online ad sales, it is growing fast. This year in the United States, advertisers are expected to spend about $2 billion on display ads bought through electronic auction-based exchanges, versus about $733 million in 2010, according to a recent report from Forrester Research. By 2017, the report estimated, that market is likely to reach $8.3 billion.

Rubicon's customers now include ABC, eBay, CareerBuilder, Glam Media, Time Inc., the Drudge Report and Zynga. Its competitors include major players like PubMatic and Google's DoubleClick ad exchange.

But Rubicon is not just a sales platform for Web site operators. It's an analytics system that uses consumer data to help sites figure out how much their visitors are worth to advertisers.

Most sites, Mr. Addante explains, compile data about their own visitors through member registration or by placing bits of computer code called cookies on people's browsers to collect information about their online activities. To those first-party profiles, Rubicon typically adds details from third-party data aggregators, like BlueKai or eXelate, such as users' sex and age, interests, estimated income range and past purchases. Finally, Rubicon applies its own analytics to estimate the fair market value of site visitors and the ad spaces they are available to see.

The whole process typically takes less than 30 milliseconds.

"All these calculations have to happen before the Web page loads," Mr. Addante says. "In our system, inventory is perishable."

The competition for pricing accuracy has made companies involved in real-time bidding among the Internet's most aggressive consumer trackers. Among the trackers setting the most cookies on the top 1,000 Web sites in the United States, for example, BlueKai was first, with 2,562 cookies, while Rubicon came in second, with 2,470, according to research conducted last month by the Berkeley Center for Law and Technology.

Consumer advocates say real-time bidding companies are acquiring and commoditizing all of that consumer data with little benefit to consumers themselves — and much digital snooping.

Mr. Addante and other industry executives disagree, saying consumers benefit by receiving ads and offers specifically relevant to them. Their systems do not invade privacy, they say, because they use numerical customer codes — not real names or other identifying details — to collect "anonymous" information about people's online activities.

For many consumers, however, that Web and search history may seem personal, especially if they visit financial or health sites. Some computer scientists argue that the customer codes assigned to online users are unique ID's, allowing companies to compile portraits about millions of people — without needing to know their names. Moreover, a few researchers have reported that many sites leak personal information, like names and addresses, to third-party trackers operating on their sites.

That means that rather than being anonymous, those customer code numbers are pseudonymous at best, some computer researchers say.

"It's like a Social Security number, a number that businesses can use to recognize you on your future visits," says Rob van Eijk, a computer science researcher at Leiden University in the Netherlands, where he is studying real-time bidding. Yet, he adds, consumers generally remain in the dark as to how automated trading systems rank and shunt them. "Envision a Kafkaesque future," he said, "where decisions are being made about you and you don't know what the criteria are based on."

Tick. Tick. Tick. Tick.

The horizontal ticker at the bottom of Turn's buy-side trading dashboard registers the groups of users available now to see ads — and lists the bids that Turn's system recommends for access to them.

The ad spaces, or impressions, sell in lots of 1,000. The price depends on variables like the size and type of ad space, the type of user, and whether the user is in an urban or rural location.

One moment, Turn's system recommends that an insurance customer bid up to $35.70 per lot being sold by Facebook Exchange, a Facebook service that auctions ad space on the social networking site, and $1.35 per lot being offered by AppNexus, another sell-side platform. That means Turn has identified Facebook's lots as "premium inventory," says Mr. Alfieri, Turn's vice president for marketing, while AppNexus is selling ads on sites where little is known about the users available to see them.

Real-time dashboards like Turn's, he says, have modernized the online ad trade in the same way that Bloomberg terminals revolutionized Wall Street trading. Ad agencies and brands can now check the intraday prices for various impressions. Many ad agencies have even created in-house "trading desks" to monitor and adjust their bids.

But Turn's dashboard is more than a real-time ticker. It's an analytics system that enables clients like insurers or car companies to identify common details among their best customer segments and then bid to show ads to people who resemble those best customers. The machine learning process gets better at pinpointing ideal audiences over the course of an ad campaign.

For example, Turn recently ran an ad campaign for a sneaker company that initially chose to buy a wide variety of impressions nationwide. But as Turn's system analyzed the early sets of results, it began to separate audiences into the kinds of people who clicked on those sneaker ads, or later searched for the shoes on their own, and those who did not. Identifying common details among those people required the system to comb through its databank of nearly a billion user profiles for each transaction.

(Like Rubicon, Turn uses consumer data from third-party data aggregators for its analyses, Mr. Alfieri said, adding that the company has hired outside software services to strip names and other details from the profiles before Turn receives them).

The results of the sneaker campaign were surprising, says Bill Demas, the chief executive of Turn.

"It turned out that Republicans in certain districts of Texas basically did not exercise. We were able to adjust the campaign to try to aim more at Democrats," Mr. Demas says. Without analyzing those user profiles, he says, "who would think that party affiliation would be an influence in advertising campaigns?"

In some ways, the consumer segmentation process is not as newfangled as it may seem. For decades in the bricks-and-mortar world, direct marketers have hired third-party data resellers to help them decide which customers should get catalogs or special offers in the mail. Real-time bidding is just a faster, smarter, more automated process for brands to find prospects likely to be the best fit for their products, says Joe Zawadzki, C.E.O. of MediaMath, a buy-side trading platform and data management company in Manhattan.

"How much is a rich person worth? To Mercedes, a lot. To a used Pinto dealer, not a lot," he says. "It's a different set of impressions for every marketer. That's where the magic happens."

But privacy advocates argue that real-time bidding is more problematic than direct mail because it often involves dozens of business-to-business companies — whose names most consumers have never heard of — collecting information and making instant decisions about them. The concern, advocates say, is that the very same automated bidding system that can distinguish coffee drinkers from, say, tea drinkers, and set different prices to show them ads, is also capable of distinguishing shopaholics or people in debt and potentially auctioning them to high-interest payday lenders.

"The reality looks like 'we know a person is a sucker and they spend a lot of money on dumb things,' " says Mr. Auerbach of the Electronic Frontier Foundation. "Advertisers will spend more money to target them, and they aren't savvy enough to know what is happening to them."

As real-time bidding gains traction, the consumer data-mining that fuels it is escalating. Yet that surge in surveillance may present a serious risk for online businesses.

The volume of data collection on the Web has surged 400 percent, from an average of 10 collections a page in 2011 to 50 a page this year, according to a study published last June by Krux, a company that helps businesses protect and monetize their consumer data. The report attributed the explosive growth to the ad industry's shift to real-time bidding.

Krux also warned Web site operators about what it called "rogue data collection." When publishers allow third parties, like real-time bidding platforms or information resellers, to collect data on their site, the report said, those partners often bring in other data miners whose practices the sites themselves cannot control. Those middlemen may use a site's proprietary data to help competitors, the report said.

"Publishers who leak data leak revenue," the report warned. "They face threats from middlemen who steal data and use it to create directly competitive audience-based offerings."

Those threats may increase as real-time bidding moves more aggressively into mobile sites and apps, entities that may collect valuable information about users' real-time locations and geographic patterns.

In May, Rubicon acquired Mobsmith, a start-up specializing in mobile ad technology. A few months later, the company announced that it was integrating real-time bidding for mobile ads into its system. Mr. Addante says he expects the industry to adopt real-time bidding for mobile ads faster than it had for desktop display ads. He also predicts that consumers will find tailored mobile ads for, say, a cafe or taxi in their vicinity, more pertinent than many Web ads tailored to them.

"I think mobile ads become more of an information provider than what is happening in display advertising where it has become a nuisance," he says.

Yet the prospect of ubiquitous real-time bidding — online, on mobile devices and eventually on Web-enabled televisions — also hastens our transition to a totally traceable society. What we read and how we spend our spare time used to be private. Now those activities are becoming windows through which marketers scrutinize, appraise and vie to influence us for a price. Soon there may be no personal spaces left for our private thoughts.

"Real-time bidding creates the possibility for companies to tag you wherever you are going, without you knowing or having the ability to influence it," says Mr. van Eijk, the computer scientist. "It is becoming a huge imbalance for the ordinary user because, in the end, the ordinary user is the product."

Marketers Are Sizing Up the Millennials

BY DIONNE SEARCEY | AUG. 21, 2014

MILLENNIALS HAVE BEEN called a lot of names. Narcissistic, lazy, indecisive. They have been labeled the boomerang generation for the many unable or unwilling to leave their parents' home, or even more negatively, the Peter Pan generation because they supposedly won't grow up.

But now marketers, manufacturers and retailers are recognizing the group's potential as something important to their bottom line: the consumers who will drive the economy in the decades ahead.

Since the 1960s — the era of "Mad Men" — the baby boom generation, born between 1946 and 1964, has dominated corporate strategies behind selling nearly everything. Still constituting one-fourth of the nation's population, baby boomers created an economy fueled by credit cards and trips to shopping malls as they came of age in a time of relative affluence. For all the rebelliousness of the '60s and early '70s, most ended up buying houses in the suburbs, eating at fast-food restaurants, and acquiring spacious minivans and S.U.V.s despite having relatively small families.

But now young adults in their 20s are moving to surpass baby boomers as the largest age group, changing the way everything is sold, even breakfast drinks and mattresses.

"Our whole consumer model is based on the baby boom," said Diane Swonk, chief economist for Mesirow Financial. Now, the coming generation is "setting up a whole new consumer model."

Perhaps the biggest change is that today's young adults — in part because they came of age in a harsher economic climate, in part because they have many more choices — are putting off major life decisions as well as the big purchases that typically go with them. As a result, their consumer behavior is unpredictable. "They've learned to live life in a different way," Ms. Swonk said.

Leslie Coronel shopping online in her dorm room at Amherst.

There are more 23-year-olds — 4.7 million of them — than any other age, according to census data from June. The second most populous age group was 24, and the third was 22. There is no official age range for millennials but the generation generally is defined as being born between the early 1980s and early 2000s. By 2020, they will account for one-third of the adult population.

At the same time, millennials are the most educated generation in American history. Far more members of this generation are going to college than of past generations.

The largest slice is now graduating and emerging in a postrecession landscape where the job market is still troubled but starting to show signs of improving. Many of the new college graduates have student debt to pay off. And wage growth for younger college graduates has risen slowly since the recession, lagging that of all full-time workers and making expensive purchases more difficult.

But they also have significant earning potential in the years to come and, because of the sheer size of the group, have the ability to reshape the economy in ways that haven't happened since the huge baby boom generation was hitting the job market and moving into first homes.

Nathan Lipsky, 23, exhibits many characteristics of his generation that are prompting upheaval in numerous industries. Though he earns a good salary in a job in the financial services industry in Kansas City, Mo., Mr. Lipsky said buying a house and getting married were not on his radar for the near future.

"Right now it's purely career-focused," said Mr. Lipsky, who lives with his parents. "This is a very selfish time in life."

Mortgage lenders and automobile manufacturers, who deal with the largest purchases most people make, have yet to figure out how to successfully tap this group of consumers. Mattress companies are another striking example.

In an article called "Meet the Millennials: Getting to Know Your Next Big Customer," the trade publication BedTimes Magazine offered tips for marketing to young adults who are stalling on traditions like marriage that in the past have prompted mattress shopping. The article advised mattress companies to sponsor a music concert or create online quizzes about mattresses.

"Tricky to sell to," the article said, "they must be approached on their own terms."

It's worth remembering, of course, that baby boomers puzzled marketers in their day as they embraced consumer crazes — Frisbees, bell bottoms and stereo systems — even though they craved self-expression and many took part in counterculture activities. They, too, were described like millennials: selfish, entitled and unwilling to grow up. Even as they entered their 30s, the writer Tom Wolfe labeled the era the "Me Decade."

"There is no strong reason to believe that millennials are dramatically different than the generations of Americans that preceded them," Jason Furman, chairman of the Council of Economic Advisers, said last month at a housing forum on how millennials have fared in the years after the recession. "Rather, it is the unlucky economic times with which they were presented that explains much of their challenge."

Still, many young adults are proving particularly baffling to marketers and researchers. While baby boomers have long exhibited consistent brand loyalty, 20-somethings "trade up and trade down," said Jeff Fromm, who runs FutureCast, a millennial trends consulting company, and wrote a book about marketing to millennials.

Last September, the fashion magazine Teen Vogue worked with Goldman Sachs in a survey of young women ages 13 to 29 to come up with a list of the most popular brands sought by the cohort. Both Target and Louis Vuitton made the top 20 list.

Leslie Coronel, who is entering her junior year at Amherst College in central Massachusetts, said she was careful to shop for most groceries at major chains where she can buy bread at a discount. Yet she often stops at the bakery at Whole Foods for more expensive treats. She does nearly all of her other shopping online, and when she goes to a clothing shop, she heads straight to the sales rack. But if she finds an expensive dress or shoes she really likes, she splurges.

Such behavior has spawned a cottage industry of consultants who collect fees from companies clamoring to figure out what this age group wants.

The Center for Generational Kinetics in Austin, Tex., was founded four years ago and has worked with about 100 clients including Mercedes-Benz, Four Seasons Hotels, General Electric and numerous retailers who want advice on how to appeal to millennial tastes.

"What worked five years ago doesn't work now in terms of marketing and selling and advertising," said Jason Dorsey, the center's chief strategy officer. "This has created a lot of urgency as more and more of these millennials enter the market and start to have money or spend money they don't have."

General Mills, one of the country's largest food companies, last year revamped its frozen pizza brand, Totino's, with black packaging and spicy flavors in an effort to appeal to millennials. The new

Totino's Bold products are marketed with zombie videos on YouTube instead of the picture of the matronly chef Rose Totino clad in red-and-white checkered apron that graced newspaper ads in the 1980s, when the target consumer was baby boomer mothers.

"This is an incredibly big part of our mission when there's an age group as large as this is," said Maria Carolina Comings, a marketing manager for General Mills.

Breakfast drinks are also experiencing millennial-related upheaval. Marketers have found that young adults want something besides orange juice or coffee in the morning. Many of them, who exercise more than their parents at that age, have energy drinks for breakfast.

PepsiCo already has responded to that change with Kickstart, a drink it created with millennials in mind that combines Mountain Dew flavor with 5 percent fruit juice. The company markets its citrus and fruit punch flavors of the caffeinated drink as a breakfast beverage.

Adapting to this new group of consumers should be worth it. While baby boomers, not surprisingly, outspend millennials by a wide margin, millennials already represent $1.3 trillion in consumer spending, out of total spending of nearly $11 trillion, according to a study by Moosylvania, a digital marketing company in St. Louis. Young adults, the study found, need a lot of reassurance but don't like to be marketed to.

"No one truly understand millennials," the researchers summarized. "Not even millennials."

Blacks Are Challenged to Buy From Black-Owned Businesses to Close Gap

BY TATIANA WALK-MORRIS | NOV. 15, 2015

CHICAGO — Should black people go out of their way to patronize black-owned business?

Maggie Anderson says they should. In 2008, with the economy in the middle of the worst downturn since the 1930s, Ms. Anderson enlisted her husband and two daughters in a yearlong plan to consume goods and services exclusively from black-owned businesses. The journey became a basis for her 2012 book, "Our Black Year," the subject of several TED talks about how to increase wealth in the African-American community, and the narrative behind a current cross-country tour aimed at spreading her gospel.

Blacks spend less money in black-owned businesses than other racial and ethnic groups spend in businesses owned by members of their groups, including Hispanics and Asians. A report by Nielsen and Essence estimates that black buying power will reach $1.3 trillion in the next few years, yet only a tiny fraction of that money is spent at black-owned businesses. Unless black people devote more attention to building wealth within the black community, Ms. Anderson and others contend, they will always be behind.

For Ms. Anderson, buying black presented multiple challenges. She purchased gas from a black-owned Citgo gas station 35 miles away from her home in Oak Park, Ill. Because that was inconvenient, she eventually bought gas cards from a black-owned store and used them at a station near her home. Finding a black-owned grocery store, bank and other establishments was more challenging than she had expected.

"When I think back on that year, driving was the least of it," said Ms. Anderson, a lawyer with a master's degree in business administration. "It was heartbreaking taking in how the West Side and the

South Side used to have so many business owners, and now most of those businesses are owned by outsiders."

Critics of Ms. Anderson's book said she was discriminating by refusing to buy from businesses owned by whites and other ethnicities. And some argued that promoting black-on-black business could do more harm than good if it discouraged black entrepreneurs from trying to serve all consumers.

But Ms. Anderson says that her goals are inclusive, and that she has also sought to encourage companies in industries like fashion, entertainment and liquor that profit from black clientele to do more to support black communities and do business with black suppliers.

"When we think about diversity, we still think about H.R. diversity," Ms. Anderson said at a public meeting here in Chicago, referring to human resources and recruiting for jobs. "It's not about H.R. diversity; it's about supplier diversity. If you want us to do business with you, you have to do business with us."

Maggie Anderson and her family spent a year buying only from black-owned businesses.

She noted that black-owned businesses employed high percentages of black people, multiplying the benefits of buying from them.

"At first, I did take it personally that people would call us racist," Ms. Anderson said. But "if we want to create jobs in the black community, we have to support black businesses."

Spurring job creation in the black community is one of her goals. A study by the Kellogg School of Management at Northwestern University found that between half a million and a million jobs could be created if higher-income black households spent only $1 of every $10 at black-owned stores and other enterprises.

"The million jobs will only happen if collectively the black community worked to invest more of their spending with black-owned businesses," Ms. Anderson said at the meeting, a stop on her $50 Billion Empowerment Tour, a 20-city tour with Eugene Mitchell, a corporate vice president and African-American market manager at New York Life. "There's a lot that we can do if we make small sacrifices."

But that is only part of the challenge. Though statistics show that black incomes and higher education rates are rising, working hard and investing more in the black community will not be enough to level the playing field, according to Darrick Hamilton, an associate professor of economics and urban policy and director of the Milano Doctoral Program at The New School in New York.

The relative dearth of black businesses stems in large part from the lack of wealth built up over generations and the limited access to capital, Mr. Hamilton said. "We often think of slavery as the only point of departure, when in fact it was many policies that took place after the Great Depression and after enduring World War II that created a white asset-based middle class," he said.

"It was government intervention that created a white, asset-based middle class," he added, "and it's going to take government intervention to create a black, asset-based middle class as well."

Findings from the Pew Research Center show that income gains for black households have not narrowed the wealth gap.

Even though African-American income growth outpaced that of whites, the median net worth of black households in 2011 was only $6,446, a decline of nearly 10 percent from 1984, when it was $7,150 in inflation-adjusted dollars. By contrast, the median net worth for whites, already far higher than for blacks, rose 11 percent to $91,405 over the same period.

On average, business equity was the second-biggest asset class among whites, after personal homes, but it was the least valuable asset for blacks, accounting for less than 4 percent on average.

Discriminatory lending practices and mishandled policies have led many blacks to distrust conventional financial institutions, Mr. Mitchell said. "For 250 years, we had no opportunity to create wealth; we created wealth for others," he said. "There's been a lot of distrust and miseducation."

Among black business owners, generating capital requires unusual creativity and initiative. Chris Brown, an entrepreneur who runs a fitness gym, an online T-shirt creation website and an online boat rental service, said running multiple ventures allowed him to generate enough revenue to create his own "bank," or pool of investment capital, rather than seeking financing elsewhere. And to succeed, he said, he looked beyond the black community.

A former Marine, Mr. Brown started with The Boot Camp Guy, a fitness center on Chicago's South Side. In addition to his service in the Marines, Mr. Brown attributes his ability to relate to customers from widely varying backgrounds to his childhood experiences traveling with his stepfather, who was an executive with the Peace Corps.

"I've found a way to break down the barrier where they're not looking at a black male," Mr. Brown said. "They're looking at a person that lived in a country that's very culturally similar to what they've experienced."

Still, subtle biases can prevent nonblack customers from patronizing black businesses. In a 2010 study, "The Visible Hand: Race and Online Market Outcomes," advertisements for a new iPod were posted online, and the ads showed the hands of a black person, a white person without a tattoo and a white person with a tattoo holding the new iPod.

The study found that discrimination was greater in markets where black and white residents were geographically isolated from one another. Black sellers were offered less money and respondents to black sellers exhibited lower trust.

For African-American communities, black support for black-owned businesses is critical to their survival, said Veranda Dickens, chairwoman of Seaway Bank, which is based in Chicago, was founded in 1965 and is now the third-largest black-owned bank in the country, behind Liberty Bank & Trust and One United Bank.

"The mission is still as important today as it was 50 years ago," Ms. Dickens said.

Ms. Anderson said she was developing Maggie's List, an online guide to help consumers find black-owned businesses, which she hopes to have running in six to eight months.

Her black year "was hard, because I tried to do it 100 percent, but there are little things that we can do to increase our spending with black-owned businesses," Ms. Anderson said. "Once you get started, it gets easier and easier."

Amazon Knows What You Buy. And It's Building a Big Ad Business From It.

BY KAREN WEISE | JAN. 20, 2019

SEATTLE — When a chain of physical therapy centers wanted new patients, it aimed online ads at people near its offices who had bought knee braces recently on Amazon.

When a financial services provider wanted to promote its retirement advisory business, it directed ads to people in their 40s and 50s who had recently ordered a personal finance book from Amazon.

And when a major credit card company wanted new customers, it targeted people who used cards from other banks on the retail site.

The advertisers found those people by using Amazon's advertising services, which leverage what the company knows better than anyone: consumers' online buying habits.

"Amazon has a really straightforward database — they know what I buy," said Daniel Knijnik, co-founder of Quartile Digital, an Amazon-focused ad agency that oversaw the ads for the clinics and retirement services. "For an advertiser, that's a dream."

Ads sold by Amazon, once a limited offering at the company, can now be considered a third major pillar of its business, along with e-commerce and cloud computing. Amazon's advertising business is worth about $125 billion, more than Nike or IBM, Morgan Stanley estimates. At its core are ads placed on Amazon.com by makers of toilet paper or soap that want to appear near product search results on the site.

But many ad agencies are particularly excited by another area of advertising that is less obvious to many consumers. The company has been steadily expanding its business of selling video or display ads — the square and rectangular ads on sites across the web — and gaining ground on the industry leaders, Google and Facebook.

In addition to knowing what people buy, Amazon also knows where people live, because they provide delivery addresses, and which credit cards they use. It knows how old their children are from their baby registries, and who has a cold, right now, from cough syrup ordered for two-hour delivery. And the company has been expanding a self-service option for ad agencies and brands to take advantage of its data on shoppers.

"That is where the insane scale can happen for the business," said John Denny, a vice president at CAVU Venture Partners, which invests in consumer brands like Bulletproof coffee and Hippeas chickpea puffs.

Major online ad networks offer different ways to target customers. A brand that sells running shirts for women might turn to Google to find people who the company believes are female and interested in running based on their search and browsing history. The company may turn to Facebook for people in a women's running group.

Many of Amazon's features are similar to those of Google or Facebook, like offering ways to target users based on their interests, searches and demographics. But Amazon's ad system can also remove a lot of the guesswork by showing ads to people who have bought the shirts on Amazon.com.

Advertisers have long run some targeted campaigns through Amazon's ad network. Many have done that by working directly with Amazon's staff, who would place their orders on their behalf. That option has historically been focused on larger brands because it requires a minimum advertising commitment. Over time, Amazon has given more advertisers and their agencies access to the self-service system to run their own targeting campaigns on and off Amazon's websites, and at a variety of spending levels.

Users of the self-service system can choose from hundreds of automated audience segments. Some of Amazon's targeting capabilities are dependent on shopping behaviors, such as "International Market Grocery Shopper" and people who have bought "Acne Treatments" in the past month, or household demographics, such as "Presence of children aged 4-6." Others are based on the media people consume on Amazon, such as "Denzel Washington Fans" or people who have recently streamed fitness and exercise videos on Amazon. The company declined to comment.

Just the Cheese, a brand run by Specialty Cheese Company in Reeseville, Wis., makes crunchy dried cheese bars that have taken off as a low-carb snack. By using algorithms to analyze how Just the Cheese's search ads performed on Amazon's site, the ad agency Quartile Digital noticed that people who searched for keto snacks and cauliflower pizza crust, both low-carb diet trends, also bought a lot of cheese bars. So Quartile ran display ads across the web targeting Amazon customers who had bought those two specific product categories. Over three months, Amazon showed the ads on websites more than six million times, which resulted in almost 22,000 clicks and more than 4,000 orders.

That 20 percent conversion rate — a sale to one out of five people who clicked on the ads — was "amazing," Mr. Knijnik said. "That is the kind of powerful granularity for building the target audiences that just Amazon can give you."

Like other ad networks, Amazon uses cookies and other technical tools to track customers from its site onto other websites. They let the company know that a person who recently bought a diet book is now reading news on CNN and could be targeted on that site with an ad for a protein bar. Amazon does not tell the advertisers who that user is, but it does serve her ads on the brand's behalf.

Last year, Amazon released a tool similar to those used by some other ad networks. That tool embeds a piece of computer code known as a pixel in ads shown on other sites, and tracks how that particular ad placement leads to customers viewing a product on Amazon or buying it outright.

"They want more branding dollars, those TV dollars; that is really part of the reason they launched that advertising attribution data," said Melissa Burdick, who worked on Amazon's ad teams before leaving to found Pacvue, which provides tools for brands to optimize Amazon ads.

Aside from shopping habits, consumers give Amazon other information that it uses to aim ads. For example, Amazon's website has a section called "Garage," where customers can submit their car's make and model information to make sure they buy parts that fit. In 2015, Amazon used Garage data to help an auto insurer target specific customers, according to a case study on its site. Now, on their own, brands can choose to show ads to drivers who have an Acura MDX as opposed to people who have an Acura TL via Amazon's ad portal.

Amazon has slowly been developing ways for brands to target their own customers and shoppers, like other ad networks have offered for a while. Advertisers can upload their own customer lists, which Amazon matches with its database, and then show ads to those customers, or other people Amazon's algorithms determine are similar.

Mr. Denny of CAVU Venture Partners pointed to one of his firm's investments, One Brands, which sells protein bars on Amazon. The company can retarget customers who looked at the product page for its birthday cake-flavored bars, as well as so-called look-alike audiences that lets One Brands find consumers whose shopping behavior Amazon has determined is similar to people who have bought the bars before.

It not only finds those customers, but Amazon automatically shows different ads to different people based on their shopping behavior. People who do a lot of research on products may see an ad that features positive product reviews, whereas those who have signed up for regular deliveries of other products in the past might see an ad offering a discount for those who "Subscribe & Save."

"Early tests are showing this is insanely powerful," Mr. Denny said. "They can do this and nobody else can come close."

SAPNA MAHESHWARI contributed reporting from New York.

How E-Commerce Sites Manipulate You Into Buying Things You May Not Want

BY JENNIFER VALENTINO-DEVRIES | JUNE 24, 2019

WHEN POTENTIAL CUSTOMERS visit the online resale store ThredUp, messages on the screen regularly tell them just how much other users of the site are saving.

"Alexandra from Anaheim just saved $222 on her order" says one message next to an image of a bright, multicolored dress. It's a common technique on shopping websites, intended to capitalize on people's desire to fit in with others and to create a "fear of missing out."

But "Alexandra from Anaheim" did not buy the dress. She does not exist. Instead, the website's code pulled combinations from a preprogrammed list of names, locations and items and presented them as actual recent purchases.

The fake messages are an example of "dark patterns," devious online techniques that manipulate users into doing things they might not otherwise choose to. They are the digital version of timeworn tactics used to influence consumer behavior, like impulse purchases placed near cash registers, or bait-and-switch ads for used cars.

Sometimes, the methods are clearly deceptive, as with ThredUp, but often they walk a fine line between manipulation and persuasion: Think of the brightly colored button that encourages you to agree to a service, while the link to opt out is hidden in a drop-down menu.

Web designers and consumers have been highlighting examples of dark patterns online since Harry Brignull, a user-experience consultant in Britain, coined the term in 2010. But interest in the tools of online influence has intensified in the past year, amid a series of high-profile revelations about Silicon Valley companies' handling of people's private information. An important element of that discussion is the notion of consent: what users are agreeing to do and share online, and how far businesses can go in leading them to make decisions.

The prevalence of dark patterns across the web is unknown, but in a study released this week, researchers from Princeton University have started to quantify the phenomenon, focusing first on retail companies. The study is the first to systematically examine a large number of sites. The researchers developed software that automatically scanned more than 10,000 sites and found that more than 1,200 of them used techniques that the authors identified as dark patterns, including ThredUp's fake notifications.

The report coincides with discussions among lawmakers about regulating technology companies, including through a bill proposed in April by Senators Deb Fischer, Republican of Nebraska, and Mark Warner, Democrat of Virginia, that is meant to limit the use of dark patterns by making some of the techniques illegal and giving the Federal Trade Commission more authority to police the practice.

"We are focused in on a problem that I think everyone recognizes," said Ms. Fischer, adding that she became interested in the problem after becoming annoyed in her personal experience with the techniques.

The legislation faces uncertain prospects, in part because of language defining dark patterns and the companies that would be subject to the new law that is ambiguous, said Woodrow Hartzog, a law and computer science professor at Northeastern University. Still, he added, it is an important first step for policymakers in discussing dark patterns.

"The important question as a policy matter is what separates a dark pattern from good old-fashioned advertising," he said. "It's a notoriously difficult line to find — what's permissible persuasion vs wrongful manipulation."

The Princeton study identified dark-pattern techniques across the web by automatically scanning the sites' text and code.

On ThredUp, for example, the researchers saw the website create the messages in April using code that arbitrarily selected combinations from a list of 100 names, 59 locations and 82 items. The New York Times replicated the results. On one day this month, the code led to messages in which "Abigail from Albuquerque" appeared to buy more than two dozen items, including dresses in sizes 2, 4, 6 and 8. On other occasions, it yielded messages showing different people "just" buying the same secondhand item days or months apart.

When asked about the notices, a ThredUp spokeswoman said in an emailed statement that the company used "real data" and that it included the fake names and locations "to be sensitive to privacy." When asked whether the messages represented actual recent purchases, the company did not respond.

The number of sites the researchers found using dark patterns underestimates the techniques' overall prevalence online, said Arunesh Mathur, a Princeton doctoral student and an author of the paper. The researchers' software focused on text, and it scanned only retail stores' pages and not travel booking sites, social media services or other areas where such tactics might be used. The study, he added, was also confined to patterns used to influence purchasing behavior, not data-sharing or other activities.

More than 160 retail sites used a tactic called "confirmshaming" that requires users to click a button that says something like "No thanks! I'd rather join the 'Pay Full Price for Things' club" if they want to avoid signing up or buying something.

More than two dozen sites used confusing messages when encouraging users to sign up for emails and other services. On a New Balance athletic apparel site, for instance, the first part of one message suggested that a user could check a box to receive emails, but on closer reading, the opposite was true. "We'd love to send you emails with offers and new products," it said, "but if you do not wish to receive these updates, please tick this box."

New Balance believes the opt-out is "legally compliant and we believe clear to consumers," Damien Leigh, senior vice president of global direct-to-consumer sales for the company, said in a statement.

But he added that the company "is always looking for ways to be as transparent as possible with consumers and will evaluate the study's insight when it is released."

About 30 sites made it easy to sign up for services but particularly hard to cancel, requiring phone calls or other procedures. The Times requires people to talk with a representative online or by phone to cancel subscriptions, but the researchers did not study it or other publishing sites.

Most sites identified by the researchers used messages that indicated that products were popular, that there were few items in stock or that products would only be available for a limited time. Some were demonstrably false, while others were unclear.

There is disagreement about whether messages about things like high demand constitute a dark pattern if they are truthful. But even those based on actual site activity are an attempt to play on consumers' known weaknesses, said Arvind Narayanan, a Princeton computer science professor and an author of the paper.

"We are not claiming that everything we categorize in the paper should be of interest to government regulators," he said. "But there should at least be more transparency about them so that online shoppers can be more aware of how their behavior is being nudged."

CHAPTER 3

Trends in Consumerism

Consumerism operates on a supply and demand cycle: Merchandisers attempt to predict consumer trends while individual consumers direct the focus of the market. From certain styles to overall attitudes toward consumption, the consumer shapes the retailer as the retailer shapes the consumer. The articles in this chapter speak to trends in consumption, from changes in attitudes and behaviors to shopping patterns.

Buying Into the Green Movement

BY ALEX WILLIAMS | JULY 1, 2007

HERE'S ONE POPULAR VISION for saving the planet: Roll out from under the sumptuous hemp-fiber sheets on your bed in the morning and pull on a pair of $245 organic cotton Levi's and an Armani biodegradable knit shirt.

Stroll from the bedroom in your eco-McMansion, with its photo-voltaic solar panels, into the kitchen remodeled with reclaimed lumber. Enter the three-car garage lighted by energy-sipping fluorescent bulbs and slip behind the wheel of your $104,000 Lexus hybrid.

Drive to the airport, where you settle in for an 8,000-mile flight — careful to buy carbon offsets beforehand — and spend a week driving golf balls made from compacted fish food at an eco-resort in the Maldives.

That vision of an eco-sensitive life as a series of choices about what to buy appeals to millions of consumers and arguably defines the current environmental movement as equal parts concern for the earth and for making a stylish statement.

Some 35 million Americans regularly buy products that claim to be earth-friendly, according to one report, everything from organic beeswax lipstick from the west Zambian rain forest to Toyota Priuses. With baby steps, more and more shoppers browse among the 60,000 products available under Home Depot's new Eco Options program.

Such choices are rendered fashionable as celebrities worried about global warming appear on the cover of Vanity Fair's "green issue," and pop stars like Kelly Clarkson and Lenny Kravitz prepare to be headline acts on July 7 at the Live Earth concerts at sites around the world.

Consumers have embraced living green, and for the most part the mainstream green movement has embraced green consumerism. But even at this moment of high visibility and impact for environmental activists, a splinter wing of the movement has begun to critique what it sometimes calls "light greens."

Critics question the notion that we can avert global warming by buying so-called earth-friendly products, from clothing and cars to homes and vacations, when the cumulative effect of our consumption remains enormous and hazardous.

"There is a very common mind-set right now which holds that all that we're going to need to do to avert the large-scale planetary catastrophes upon us is make slightly different shopping decisions," said Alex Steffen, the executive editor of Worldchanging.com, a Web site devoted to sustainability issues.

The genuine solution, he and other critics say, is to significantly reduce one's consumption of goods and resources. It's not enough to build a vacation home of recycled lumber; the real way to reduce one's carbon footprint is to only own one home.

Buying a hybrid car won't help if it's the aforementioned Lexus, the luxury LS 600h L model, which gets 22 miles to the gallon on the highway; the Toyota Yaris ($11,000) gets 40 highway miles a gallon with a standard gasoline engine.

It's as though the millions of people whom environmentalists have successfully prodded to be concerned about climate change are experiencing a SnackWell's moment: confronted with a box of fat-free devil's food chocolate cookies, which seem deliciously guilt-free, they consume the entire box, avoiding any fats but loading up on calories.

The issue of green shopping is highlighting a division in the environmental movement: "the old-school environmentalism of self-abnegation versus this camp of buying your way into heaven," said Chip Giller, the founder of Grist.org, an online environmental blog that claims a monthly readership of 800,000. "Over even the last couple of months, there is more concern growing within the traditional camp about the Cosmo-izing of the green movement — '55 great ways to look eco-sexy,' " he said. "Among traditional greens, there is concern that too much of the population thinks there's an easy way out."

The criticisms have appeared quietly in some environmental publications and on the Web.

George Black, an editor and a columnist at OnEarth, a quarterly journal of the Natural Resources Defense Council, recently summed up the explosion of high-style green consumer items and articles of the sort that proclaim "green is the new black," that is, a fashion trend, as "eco-narcissism."

Paul Hawken, an author and longtime environmental activist, said the current boom in earth-friendly products offers a false promise. "Green consumerism is an oxymoronic phrase," he said. He blamed the news media and marketers for turning environmentalism into fashion and distracting from serious issues.

"We turn toward the consumption part because that's where the money is," Mr. Hawken said. "We tend not to look at the 'less' part. So you get these anomalies like 10,000-foot 'green' homes being built by a hedge fund manager in Aspen. Or 'green' fashion shows. Fashion is the deliberate inculcation of obsolescence."

A second home, complete with solar panels and constructed with salvaged lumber, in Edgartown, Mass.

He added: "The fruit at Whole Foods in winter, flown in from Chile on a 747 — it's a complete joke. The idea that we should have raspberries in January, it doesn't matter if they're organic. It's diabolically stupid."

Environmentalists say some products marketed as green may pump more carbon into the atmosphere than choosing something more modest, or simply nothing at all. Along those lines, a company called PlayEngine sells a 19-inch widescreen L.C.D. set whose "sustainable bamboo" case is represented as an earth-friendly alternative to plastic.

But it may be better to keep your old cathode-tube set instead, according to "The Live Earth Global Warming Survival Handbook," because older sets use less power than plasma or L.C.D. screens. (Televisions account for about 4 percent of energy consumption in the United States, the handbook says.)

"The assumption that by buying anything, whether green or not, we're solving the problem is a misperception," said Michael Ableman, an environmental author and long-time organic farmer. "Consuming is a significant part of the problem to begin with. Maybe the solution is instead of buying five pairs of organic cotton jeans, buy one pair of regular jeans instead."

For the most part, the critiques of green consumption have come from individual activists, not from mainstream environmental groups like the Sierra Club, Greenpeace and the Rainforest Action Network. The latest issue of Sierra, the magazine of the Sierra Club, has articles hailing an "ecofriendly mall" featuring sustainable clothing (under development in Chicago) and credit cards that rack up carbon offsets for every purchase, as well as sustainably-harvested caviar and the celebrity-friendly Tango electric sports car (a top-of-the-line model is $108,000).

One reason mainstream groups may be wary of criticizing Americans' consumption is that before the latest era of green chic, these large organizations endured years in which their warnings about climate change were scarcely heard.

Much of the public had turned away from the Carter-era environmental message of sacrifice, which included turning down the thermostat, driving smaller cars and carrying a cloth "Save-a-Tree" tote to the supermarket.

Now that environmentalism is high profile, thanks in part to the success of "An Inconvenient Truth," the 2006 documentary featuring Al Gore, mainstream greens, for the most part, say that buying products promoted as eco-friendly is a good first step.

"After you buy the compact fluorescent bulbs," said Michael Brune, the executive director of the Rainforest Action Network, "you can move on to greater goals like banding together politically to shut down coal-fired power plants."

John Passacantando, the executive director of Greenpeace USA, argued that green consumerism has been a way for Wal-Mart shoppers to get over the old stereotypes of environmentalists as "tree-hugging hippies" and contribute in their own way.

This is crucial, he said, given the widespread nature of the global warming challenge. "You need Wal-Mart and Joe Six-Pack and mayors and taxi drivers," he said. "You need participation on a wide front."

It is not just ecology activists with one foot in the 1970s, though, who have taken issue with the consumerist personality of the "light green" movement. Anti-consumerist fervor burns hotly among some activists who came of age under the influence of noisy, disruptive anti-globalization protests.

Last year, a San Francisco group called the Compact made headlines with a vow to live the entire year without buying anything but bare essentials like medicine and food. A year in, the original 10 "mostly" made it, said Rachel Kesel, 26, a founder. The movement claims some 8,300 adherents throughout the country and in places as distant as Singapore and Iceland.

"The more that I'm engaged in this, the more annoyed I get with things like 'shop against climate change' and these kind of attitudes," said Ms. Kesel, who continues her shopping strike and counts a new pair of running shoes — she's a dog-walker by trade — as among her limited purchases in 18 months.

"It's hysterical," she said. "You're telling people to consume more in order to reduce impact."

For some, the very debate over how much difference they should try to make in their own lives is a distraction. They despair of individual consumers being responsible for saving the earth from climate change and want to see action from political leaders around the world.

Individual consumers may choose more fuel-efficient cars, but a far greater effect may be felt when fuel-efficiency standards are raised for all of the industry, as the Senate voted to do on June 21, the first significant rise in mileage standards in more than two decades.

"A legitimate beef that people have with green consumerism is, at end of the day, the things causing climate change are more caused by politics and the economy than individual behavior," said Michel Gelobter, a former professor of environmental policy at Rutgers who is now president of Redefining Progress, a nonprofit policy group that promotes sustainable living.

"A lot of what we need to do doesn't have to do with what you put in your shopping basket," he said. "It has to do with mass transit, housing density. It has to do with the war and subsidies for the coal and fossil fuel industry."

In fact, those light-green environmentalists who chose not to lecture about sacrifice and promote the trendiness of eco-sensitive products may be on to something.

Michael Shellenberger, a partner at American Environics, a market research firm in Oakland, Calif., said that his company ran a series of focus groups in April for the environmental group Earthjustice, and was surprised by the results.

People considered their trip down the Eco Options aisles at Home Depot a beginning, not an end point.

"We didn't find that people felt that their consumption gave them a pass, so to speak," Mr. Shellenberger said. "They knew what they were doing wasn't going to deal with the problems, and these little consumer things won't add up. But they do it as a practice of mindfulness. They didn't see it as antithetical to political action. Folks who were engaged in these green practices were actually becoming more committed to more transformative political action on global warming."

What Nail Polish Sales Tell Us About the Economy

COLUMN | BY ADAM DAVIDSON | DEC. 14, 2011

It's the Economy is a column about how economics can explain the world.

ECONOMICS IS ALL about consumption. People either spend money now or they use financial instruments — like bonds, stocks and savings accounts — so they can spend more later. A healthy economy is largely a result of a reasonable balance between consumption today and consumption deferred, and it's pretty clear that balance has been ridiculously out of whack for a while.

Our current problem is that much of the world has shifted rapidly from consuming way more than it could afford to consuming far less. The subsequent whiplash has left many people (and, in some cases, entire countries) broke, unemployed and deeply pessimistic about the future. And while we can measure stock prices and bond rates, the key factor that determines consumption and, therefore, the health of the economy, lies in our psychology. Economists believe that what we feel about the state of the economy is best revealed not through what we say in surveys but rather through what we buy and exactly how much of it. There's a lot of data available, though none come with a prepackaged psychological narrative attached. So analysts do the best they can, combing through our national shopping lists hoping to uncover clues. Sometimes they find remarkably helpful information in very unlikely places.

They also uncover plenty of cute facts that mean little. Consider this: 2011 was a banner year for the sale of insanely expensive fine wines at auction. Someone at a Christie's auction in Hong Kong, for example, bought 12 bottles of 1985 Romanee-Conti for a bit more than $150,000, or about $600 per sip. And the grand lesson this teaches us about the overall economy is ... absolutely nothing. There's some meaning in this anecdote about how the superrich — especially the

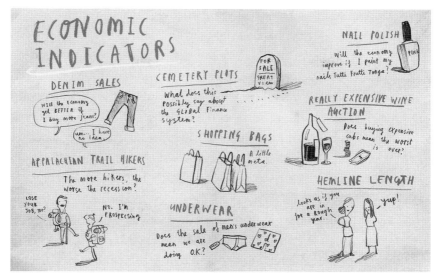

ECONOMIC INDICATORS

DENIM SALES
Will the economy get BETTER if I buy more jeans?
um... I have no idea.

APPALACHIAN TRAIL HIKERS
The more hikers, the worse the recession?
LOSE YOUR JOB, TOO?
NO. I'm PROSPECTING

CEMETERY PLOTS
FOR SALE GREAT VIEW
What does this possibly say about the GLoBal Finance system?

SHOPPING BAGS
A little meta.

UNDERWEAR
Does the sale of men's underwear mean we are doing O.K.?

NAIL POLISH
Will the economy improve if I paint my nails Tutti Frutti Tonga?
PINK

REALLY EXPENSIVE WINE AUCTION
Does buying expensive cabs mean the worst is over?

HEMLINE LENGTH
looks as if you are in for a Rough year.
yup!

ILLUSTRATION BY OLIVER JEFFERS

newly superrich in China — are doing far better than the rest of us. But that can't help us figure out if we're headed for a double dip, a stagnant decade or a sudden rebound.

To figure out what our buying behavior says about the U.S. economy's future, we have to understand what's going on in the middle class, the 50-percenters. And to figure this out, my colleagues and I at NPR's "Planet Money" went searching for as many shopping-based indicators as we could find, hoping some would unlock a hidden story about what Americans are feeling and where the country is headed.

The results were mixed, but we did uncover some ominous signs. Lipstick sales used to go up when the economy went down, perhaps because women were searching for a cheap pick-me-up or an edge in a job interview. For reasons nobody quite understands, the lipstick indicator doesn't hold up anymore, though nail polish sales now seem to reflect the economy very clearly (albeit inversely). A rise in nail polish sales indicates that we're searching for bargain luxuries as the economy craters — and sales of nail polish are way up right now. Women's underwear sales are down, which historically suggests intense frugality and more rough times ahead.

But we were encouraged by the number of optimistic indicators we uncovered. There is good news in cemetery plot sales. They seem to have peaked a couple years ago when desperate families were unloading unused holes in the ground (though cremation numbers are rising). Sales of cardboard boxes, because everything from electronics to clothing is packaged in them, should also be a strong indicator of economic rejuvenation. (Current production — enough to paper over the entire state of Maryland — portends recovery.) Sales of men's underwear, one of Alan Greenspan's favorite metrics for predicting growth, are also up. Sales of cheap spirits, which soared during the worst of the recession (people need an affordable way to self-medicate), have now stabilized, meaning, at the very least, that people can now afford better liquor.

Of all the indicators we looked at, one of the most consistently accurate was Champagne sales. The amount of French Champagne that Americans consume has predicted — with nearly 90 percent accuracy — the average American income one year later. Apparently, when we pop a Champagne cork, we know that good times are ahead. Champagne sales hurtled upward twice in recent history — at the peak of the Internet bubble in 1999 and during the heyday of the housing bubble in 2007. These were both followed by slowdowns as fewer people found reason to celebrate.

There are so many indicators to choose from that you could glean just about anything regarding our economic future. In fact, the most telling indicator appears to be the sheer number of indicators themselves. Americans now have so many seductive things they can buy that there are ample consumer options no matter what we feel. Partly as a result, savings — known in economics as deferred consumption — have fallen steadily for more than 30 years, from a high of nearly 12 percent of income. It kissed zero before a tiny uptick in the past couple years.

The decline of the savings rate is particularly troubling because it is consistent through busts *and* booms. During the fast growth of the late 1990s and mid-2000s, and the dark times that followed, people have been choosing to spend more and save less than ever before. Paradoxically, this happened just as pensions have been disappearing and life spans have been increasing. It suggests that Americans are so caught up in every short-term enthusiasm or agony that they haven't thought enough about long-term fiscal health.

When the dust clears from the current crisis in a year or two or 10, it will probably become obvious that the recent decades were a giddy consumption mirage fueled, in part, by free-flowing foreign debt. The world won't lend the United States money for nothing forever (though, downgrade aside, nobody has told the world that yet), and the country can't keep buying a lot more from everyone else than it is able to sell them. America will, most likely, need to find a more normal, sustainable level of consumption, and that's exactly the problem. We don't know what normal consumption looks like. Over much of the last few decades, we gave in to every shopping whim, with little thought to the future, except for those times we were so dispirited, we wouldn't spend at all. What does a reasonable balance between consumption now and consumption deferred actually look like? That's what we need to figure out.

ADAM DAVIDSON is the co-founder of NPR's Planet Money, a podcast, blog, and radio series heard on "Morning Edition," "All Things Considered" and "This American Life."

In Pursuit of Taste, en Masse

BY J. PEDER ZANE | FEB. 11, 2013

AMERICANS DIDN'T ALWAYS ask so many questions or expect so much in their quest for enjoyment. It was enough for them simply to savor a good cigar, a nice bottle of wine or a tasty morsel of cheese.

Not anymore. Driven by a relentless quest for "the best," we increasingly see every item we place in our grocery basket or Internet shopping cart as a reflection of our discrimination and taste. We are not consumers. We have a higher calling. We are connoisseurs.

Connoisseurship has never been more popular. Long confined to the serious appreciation of high art and classical music, it is now applied to an endless cascade of pursuits. Leading publications, including The New York Times, routinely discuss the connoisseurship of coffee, cupcakes and craft beers; of cars, watches, fountain pens, lunchboxes, stereo systems and computers; of tacos, pizza, pickles, chocolate, mayonnaise, cutlery and light (yes, light, which is not to be confused with the specialized connoisseurship of lighting). And the Grateful Dead, of course.

This democratization of connoisseurship is somewhat surprising since as recently as the social upheavals of the 1960s and '70s connoisseurship was a "dirty word" — considered "elitist, artificial, subjective and mostly imaginary," said Laurence B. Kanter, chief curator of the Yale University Art Gallery. Today, it is a vital expression of how many of us want to see, and distinguish, ourselves.

As its wide embrace opens a window onto the culture and psychology of contemporary America, it raises an intriguing question: If almost anything can be an object of connoisseurship — and if, by implication, almost anyone can be a connoisseur — does the concept still suggest the fine and rare qualities that make it so appealing?

There were probably Neanderthals who tried to distinguish themselves through their exquisite taste in cave drawings. But the word connoisseur was not coined until the 18th century — in France, of course, as a symbol of the Enlightenment's increasingly scientific approach to knowledge.

At a time when precious little was known about the provenance of many works of art, early connoisseurs developed evaluative tools — for example, identifying an artist's typical subject matter, use of color and use of light — to authenticate works by revered masters and to debunk pretenders to the pedestal.

"Works of art do not carry a guarantee," said Dr. Kanter. "It has always been the job of the connoisseur to question, investigate, refine the received wisdom of earlier generations."

As the aristocracy declined and the bourgeoisie enjoyed new wealth, especially after the Napoleonic upheavals, the number of people who could afford art expanded, as did the types of art they were interested in. Connoisseurship grew in response to the need for authoritative guidance in a changing world. In the 19th century, connoisseurs helped reassess the works of forgotten artists, like Giotto, Fra Angelico and Botticelli, who are now considered canonical. They studied and appraised ignored forms like German woodcuts, French porcelain and English statuary.

Contemporary efforts to apply connoisseurship to a host of far-flung fields are consistent with this history. "Our definition of quality continues to expand and mature," Dr. Kanter said, "so it makes sense that we can talk now about connoisseurs not just of art but also of rap music, comic books and Scotch. Connoisseurship is not about objects; it's a process of thinking about and making distinctions among things."

True connoisseurs — and this is what makes the label so appealing — do not merely possess knowledge, like scholars. They possess a sixth sense called taste. They are renowned for the unerring judgment of their discerning eye. They are celebrated because of their rare talent — their gift — for identifying and appreciating subtle, often hidden, qualities.

Despite its expanded applications, connoisseurship still revolves around art, if we define art broadly as things that are more than the sum of their parts because they offer the possibility of transcendence. We do not speak of connoisseurs of nature (which can transport us) or diapers (which are simply useful). But no one blinks when we apply the term to wine, food or literary forms like comic books, because these are believed to offer deeper experiences to those who can gain access to them. Generally speaking, almost anyone can become an expert, but connoisseurship means we're special.

If connoisseurship is a way of thinking, its rising popularity reflects the fact that people have so many more things to think about. Robert H. Frank, a professor of economics at Cornell whose books include "Luxury Fever: Why Money Fails to Satisfy in an Era of Excess," noted that the British economist John Maynard Keynes worried during the 1920s and '30s that rising productivity would lead people to work less as it became easier to satisfy their basic needs.

"It's funny," Dr. Frank said, "that someone as smart as he was didn't realize that we would invent a million new things to spend our money on and create higher and higher standards of quality for those products that would cost more and more."

Hence the $5 cup of coffee and the $8 pickle.

In the dark ages before arugula, most supermarkets seemed to carry only one type of lettuce, iceberg, and apples were either green or red. In 1945, the average grocer carried about 5,000 products; today, that number is more than 40,000, according to Paul B. Ellickson, a professor of economics and marketing at the University of Rochester.

In addition, the Internet has made millions of other options just a mouse click away. Easy access to higher-quality products opens new avenues of connoisseurship — gorau glas cheese is more interesting, more provocative, than Velveeta. But it also presents us with a mind-numbing series of choices. In this context, connoisseurship is a coping strategy. When we say we want "the best," we winnow our options, focusing our attention on a small sample of highly regarded items.

Put another way, rising connoisseurship is a response to life in an age of information shaped by consumerism. As ideas increasingly become the coin of the realm, people distinguish themselves by what they know. An important way to demonstrate this is through what they buy.

It is a form of conspicuous consumption that puts less emphasis on an item's price tag — craft beers aren't that expensive — than on its perceived cachet. In hoisting a Tripel brewed by Belgian monks, the drinker is telling the world: I know which ale to quaff. As, in all fairness, he enjoys a very tasty beverage.

Ironically, many items celebrated as examples of connoisseurship — handcrafted, small-batch, artisanal products — are themselves a reaction against the mass production trends of the global consumer society that shapes us. Just as art connoisseurs authenticate paintings, others seek wines and cheese and cupcakes that seem mystically authentic.

"A lot of what gets called connoisseurship is really just snobbery," said Thomas Frank, who has dissected modern consumer culture in books like "Commodify Your Dissent," which he edited with Matt Weiland, and "The Conquest of Cool." "It's not about the search for quality, but buying things that make you feel good about yourself. It's about standing apart from the crowd, demonstrating knowledge, hipness."

The rub is that, as access to knowledge through a Google search has become synonymous with possessing knowledge, fewer and fewer people seem to have the inclination or patience to become true connoisseurs. How many people, after all, have the time to make oodles of money and master the worlds of craft beer, cheese, wines and everything else people in the know must know?

In response, most people outsource connoisseurship, turning to actual connoisseurs for guidance. "Many people want the patina of connoisseurship on the cheap," said Barry Schwartz, a professor of social theory and social action at Swarthmore College. "So they contract out the decision-making process. My guess is that a tiny fraction of people who are true connoisseurs of wine — and there are some — don't make enough money to buy a $500 bottle of wine."

As Steven Jenkins, an expert on cheese and other products at Fairway Market in New York, recently told a reporter for The New York Times: "The customer has no idea what he or she wants. The customer is dying to be told what they want."

People have always relied on connoisseurs for guidance. What is different today is the idea — suggested by journalists and marketers intent on flattering their customers — that people can become paragons of taste simply by taking someone else's advice.

Dr. Schwartz said this could be a wise strategy. Consumers may not get the pleasures of deep knowledge, but they also avoid the angst. "You get the benefits of discernment without paying the psychological price" of having to make difficult choices and distinctions, he said. "You're happy because you've been told what to get and don't know any better."

This psychological dimension is essential to understanding connoisseurship, said Dan Ariely, a professor of psychology and behavioral economics at Duke University whose books include "Predictably Irrational." While recognizing that a small handful of people are true connoisseurs, he said his experiments with people interested in wine revealed a startling lack of discernment.

In one experiment, Dr. Ariely asked people to taste and write descriptions of four wines. He waited 10 minutes and then gave them a blind taste test, asking them to match the wines to their descriptions. For the most part, they couldn't.

In another experiment, he used food coloring to make white wine appear red. The participants, he said, "rated it highly in terms of tannins, complexity" and other general characteristics of red wine.

Dr. Ariely's work dovetails with other experiments that have found, for instance, that many people cannot tell the difference between foie gras and dog food in blind taste tests.

Even connoisseurs have a hard time getting it right. Echoing a famous blind taste test of wines from California and France in 1976, known as the Judgment of Paris, nine wine experts gathered at

Princeton University in 2012 to compare revered wines from France with wines from New Jersey that cost, on average, about 5 percent as much. Not only did the experts give vastly different scores for many of the wines, but they rated the Garden State wines on a par with their costly French counterparts.

Dr. Ariely said these results did not necessarily debunk the notion of connoisseurship. "Whether we can actually tell the difference between cheap and expensive wine may be less important than whether we think that we can," he said. "We might actually experience more pleasure when drinking an expensive wine, enjoy it more, because we're slowing down, savoring it, paying more attention to its qualities."

Which, as it turns out, is a hallmark of connoisseurship.

Black Friday Shopping Shifts Online as Stores See Less Foot Traffic

BY HIROKO TABUCHI | NOV. 27, 2015

IN SHOPS ACROSS the country, including the empty malls of Georgia and the "not too crazy" crowds at struggling J. Crew, the relative calm that accompanied Black Friday shopping this year belied a frenzy for deals — many of them on the web.

EBay boasted that it was selling two hoverboards, the "it" item of the season, every minute. Walmart said it had sold so many movies that it would take close to 3,000 years to watch all of them; many of its sales were online.

Adobe, which tracked more than 180 million visits to over 4,500 United States retail websites this Thanksgiving, said shoppers spent $1.73 billion online on Thursday — or 22 percent more than 2014. Almost 60 percent of the traffic came from mobile devices.

Early online data for Black Friday showed less oomph. But then online sales grew about 15 percent between midnight and 11 a.m. on Friday compared with the same time frame last year, with shoppers spending $822 million during that time period. Adobe expects Black Friday to generate $2.6 billion in total online sales, a 14 percent increase compared with the same day last year.

Brick-and-mortar stores saw less action. A preliminary reading of Black Friday by Retail Metrics declared traffic across apparel and department stores "uninspiring." The analytics company now expects November sales at major retailers to fall by 0.9 percent over all.

At Amazon, it was another matter.

By mid-Friday, sales at Amazon were estimated to have jumped 19.6 percent this Black Friday compared to last year, according to the e-commerce analytics company, ChannelAdvisor. Google Shopping grew 26.42 percent, ChannelAdvisor said, albeit from a smaller base.

According to Adobe, many of the top sellers online were electronics, including the Samsung 4K TV, Sony PlayStation 4, iPad Air 2 and Xbox One. Another strong category was toys. Lego Dimensions, Barbie Dream House and the BB-8 droid robot from the new "Star Wars" film sold out online.

Discounts averaging 26 percent off were driving higher sales this year, Adobe said, and average online purchases rose 5 percent from last year to $162. Doorbuster sales made up about 40 percent of sales volume.

Mickey Mericle, Adobe's vice president of marketing insights and analytics, said that this holiday shoppers seemed to finally be using their mobile devices not just to browse, but to make purchases.

"We've always seen that there's a higher degree of browsing on phones, but people reported that there were still barriers to purchasing on the phones," she said. "They didn't have their credit card info in there, and they didn't want to type that in, or maybe they couldn't see the product as well as they wanted to."

But that gap seemed to be narrowing, she said. Adobe had expected to see 29 cents on the dollar of transactions through mobile devices — but the company saw 37 cents on the dollar on mobile.

"What I suspect is happening is that people as they are shopping using their mobile device, they already have their info in there. They don't have to enter info this year," she said. The rise of mobile wallets, like PayPal or Apple Pay, was also making mobile shopping easier, she said.

At brick-and-mortar stores, foot traffic was declining as consumers increasingly shifted shopping online, Ken Perkins, a research analyst at Retail Metrics, wrote in a note. This also allowed shoppers to do in-depth research, so that even if they ultimately bought some items in store, shoppers would make a beeline for their sought-after item, without staying to browse other shelves or departments, he said.

Consumers are also spending more on restaurants, sports events, concerts, travel and services like spas. And both in stores and online, retailers benefited from earlier shopping with many starting offering deals soon after Halloween, he said.

Still, consumers appear to be more financially secure this holiday season than they have been at any time since the financial crisis. Gas prices are down, and savings rates are on the rise. The job market remains strong.

Over all, holiday spending is expected to grow at a far slower pace. The National Retail Federation, a trade group, expects retail sales online and in stores in November and December to rise at a rate of 3.7 percent, to $630 billion — slightly less than last year's 4.1 percent gain.

Walmart said that more than 25 million customers had found store maps and its Black Friday circulars online and on mobile, and that tens of millions had "visited our digital and physical aisles."

Target reported "some of the best days we've seen on Target.com," and said it expected to see demand continue through the weekend into December, on strong sales of Star Wars and Apple products, as well as its exclusive version of Adele's new album.

One retailer with high stakes riding on this holiday season is J. Crew, whose sales slump has sent its bonds into a downward spiral, sparking talk of a possible debt restructuring.

Middle-of-the-road stores like J. Crew and Banana Republic have struggled in an increasingly polarized market dominated on one end by the likes of H&M and Zara, which offer a high turnover of styles at far more competitive prices, and on the other by more high-end, luxury or specialty brands, like The Row or Everlane.

At the J. Crew at the Walt Whitman Shops in Huntington, N.Y. — where signs advertised up to 50 percent off in the sale section — Nancy Moley, a personal stylist, said Black Friday was going "comfortably, not crazy."

Kathy Reinertsen and her daughter Hannah said that J. Crew's Black Friday prices were still too high.

"They weren't worth it," Ms. Reinertsen said.

ADRIANE QUINLAN in Decatur, Ga., and **ARIELLE DOLLINGER** in Huntington Village, N.Y., contributed reporting.

The Oppressive Gospel of 'Minimalism'

ESSAY | BY KYLE CHAYKA | JULY 26, 2016

IT HAS BECOME an ostentatious ritual of consumerist self-sacrifice; people who have it all now seem to prefer having nothing at all. And, as with watching birds or going Paleo, talking about the material purge is just as important as actually doing it. So there are blog posts — in which you can see minimalism's can-do optimism curdle into something tyrannical.

A recent account, called "How Minimalism Brought Me Freedom and Joy," is emblematic of the budding genre, from its author (a wealthy serial entrepreneur, James Altucher) to its thesis (own fewer things, mostly gadgets) to its one-sentence paragraphs. Altucher explains that he gave up his permanent home, life goals and negative emotions. He threw away his college diploma, which had been gathering dust in storage. ("I don't hold onto all the things society tells me to hold onto.") He now carries nothing but a bag of clothes and a backpack containing a computer, an iPad and a smartphone. "I have zero other possessions," he writes, and thanks to this, he has found peace as a wandering techno-ascetic — Silicon Valley's version of Zen monkhood.

Despite its connotations of absence, "minimalism" has been popping up everywhere lately, like a bright algae bloom in the murk of postrecession America. From tiny houses to microapartments to monochromatic clothing to interior-decorating trends — picture white walls interrupted only by succulents — less now goes further than ever. It's easy to feel overwhelmed by the minimalism glut, as the word can be applied to just about anything. The nearly four million images tagged #minimalism on Instagram include white sneakers, clouds, the works of Mondrian, neon signs, crumbling brick walls and grassy fields. So long as it's stylishly austere, it seems, it's minimalist.

Part pop philosophy and part aesthetic, minimalism presents a cure-all for a certain sense of capitalist overindulgence. Maybe we have a hangover from pre-recession excess — McMansions, S.U.V.s, neon cocktails, fusion cuisine — and minimalism is the salutary tonic. Or perhaps it's a method of coping with recession-induced austerity, a collective spiritual and cultural cleanse because we've been forced to consume less anyway. But as an outgrowth of a peculiarly American (that is to say, paradoxical and self-defeating) brand of Puritanical asceticism, this new minimalist lifestyle always seems to end in enabling new modes of consumption, a veritable excess of less. It's not really minimal at all.

The word's meaning wasn't entirely literal when it first came into being; "minimalism" was popularized in 1965 as an insult. In an essay for Arts Magazine, the British philosopher Richard Wollheim used it to describe a group of artists whose work was characterized by "minimal art content" — that is, a lack of art. Arranging bricks on a gallery floor (as Carl Andre did) or manufacturing metal boxes (Donald Judd) or

stores in rural areas, according to Barbara Denham, a senior economist at Reis, a real estate data and analytics firm.

Jack Kleinhenz, the chief economist at the National Retail Federation, does not discount the magnitude of the transformation that is occurring in retail, but cautioned that the monthly job figures are also highly subject to temporary vagaries. "One of the challenges we have at this time of the year is the quirkiness of seasonal forces," he said.

An unexpectedly warm February and snowy March and the late arrival of Easter could have elbowed the numbers in an uncharacteristic way.

The retail employment number, he said, does not necessarily "translate into backsliding of retail sales."

Diane Swonk, the chief executive of DS Economics in Chicago, agreed. The falloff in hiring "is not a reflection of a consumer that can't spend, but rather of how they spend," she said. "Retail is one of the largest employers in the country, and it's going to go through a pretty massive secular restructuring. We shop differently now, and no one has the right model."

Most shopping is still done in person rather than online, but shopping patterns are shifting. Ms. Swonk mentioned research that shows consumers like to buy online but return things to bricks-and-mortar stores.

"Clearly, it's just not one or the other, not just bricks or clicks," she said. But the marketplace is rapidly changing and retailers "are not sure what the endgame is."

E-commerce may cause a drop in retail jobs, but a rise in warehouse, distribution and transportation jobs.

At the same time, consumers have not only been changing how they shop, but what they buy. Ms. Denham noted that while the entire retail sector ended up down nearly 30,000 jobs, the restaurant industry showed a gain of 20,000 in March on top of steady previous growth.

"There's been a shift in consumer spending from things to experiences," she said, "that's why restaurants are doing so well."

Holiday Spending Should Be Strong. And Then?

BY BEN CASSELMAN | NOV. 22, 2018

Consumer confidence points to open pocketbooks in the short run. Trade tensions, market upheaval and other factors may make the new year less bright.

AMERICANS ARE UPBEAT about the economy heading into the holiday shopping season. But that good cheer may not last long.

With the lowest unemployment rate in nearly half a century, and wage growth starting to pick up, economists expect shoppers to open their wallets. A survey by the National Retail Federation, a trade group, points to 4.1 percent more holiday spending than last year, and some forecasters expect even stronger growth. Measures of consumer confidence are near post-recession highs.

"You see momentum going into the season, cutting across a large range of categories," said Stephen Sadove, a former Saks Fifth Avenue chief who is now a senior adviser for Mastercard. "It's probably the healthiest growth we've seen in the past half-dozen years."

But those projections predate the latest round of steep stock-market declines, which this week pushed the S&P 500 index into negative territory for the year.

It's too soon to say whether the drop will rattle consumers. But even before the sell-off, many economists were warning that a combination of factors — including rising interest rates, a weakening housing market and a new round of tariffs set to take effect in January — could begin to slow down the economy in 2019.

CONSUMERS ARE FEELING GOOD.

Last year's holiday season was the best for retailers in more than a decade. Americans are feeling even better this year.

Thirty-seven percent of Americans say their finances are in better shape than they were a year ago, while 17 percent say they are worse off, according to a survey conducted for The New York Times in early November by the online research platform SurveyMonkey. Last November, just 28 percent said they were better off.

Consumers say they are feeling even more positive about the future. Forty-one percent expect to be better off financially a year from now — versus just 14 percent who expect to be worse off — and a majority of survey respondents said "continuous good times economically" were in store over the next five years.

Other surveys show similar optimism. The University of Michigan on Wednesday reported that consumer sentiment had ticked down slightly in November but that the index remained high by historical standards.

That confidence is leading consumers to loosen their purse strings, said Diane Swonk, an economist for the accounting firm Grant Thornton. She noted that spending was up in discretionary categories like restaurant meals, travel and clothing.

"Consumers are dressing up and stepping out a bit," Ms. Swonk said. "They've got money for discretionary spending, they're traveling a lot."

LOW GASOLINE PRICES MAY PROVIDE A DIVIDEND.

Consumers have plenty of reasons for feeling good. Economic growth is on track for its best annual performance since 2005. And crucially, the tight labor market at last appears to be translating into faster wage growth for workers. Average hourly earnings were up 3.1 percent in October from a year earlier, their fastest growth since before the recession.

Households are also getting help from gasoline prices, which have fallen sharply in the last month after rising earlier in the year.

"If gas prices go down, it basically acts like a tax cut," said Joseph Song, an economist for Bank of America Merrill Lynch.

Then there is the actual tax cut. The $1.5 trillion tax law that Republicans passed last year helped pump up consumer spending earlier this year, and economists said the effect is lingering into this holiday season. Over all, households' finances are in their strongest shape in years, with low levels of debt and rising after-tax income.

BUT WARNING SIGNALS ARE FLASHING.

United States gross domestic product has posted two straight quarters of strong growth, driven largely by robust consumer spending. Most economists expect that growth to slow in the final three months of the year as the effects of the tax cuts fade.

"There's a very clear spike in sales in the middle of the year obviously driven by the tax cuts, and there's an equally clear reversal in the second half of the year," said Ian Shepherdson, an economist for Pantheon Macroeconomics, a research firm. "It's the sugar rush followed by the comedown."

That slowdown, by itself, isn't much cause for concern, Mr. Shepherdson said. But there are other hints of trouble on the horizon. The housing market has slowed markedly this year, as interest rates have risen and prices have outstripped income growth. And additional tariffs on Chinese goods are set to take effect in January, which could push up consumer prices.

"Consumers are at the heart of what's gone right in the economy the past couple years, and I think they're going to be the biggest contributor to the slowdown," said James Bohnaker, an economist for IHS, a research firm.

Those concerns may be part of what has driven the stock market's recent drop. Retail stocks fell on Tuesday despite strong results, as investors worried that rising costs could eat into earnings.

The market turmoil could affect consumer sentiment, especially among wealthier households more likely to own stocks. The University of Michigan survey found that confidence fell more among higher-earning households in November.

But falling share prices are unlikely to hurt holiday sales much, Mr. Song said. Most Americans don't own stocks outside of their retirement accounts, and many have already set their holiday budgets — or have even begun to shop. A Bank of America survey found that about 20 percent of consumers started their holiday shopping before November, and 67 percent said they planned to shop over the extended Thanksgiving weekend.

"I have a tough time really seeing this hurting consumer spending," Mr. Song said of the market declines. "A lot of the shopping is already baked in."

AND FOR SOME, THE ELECTION WAS A DAMPER.

Ever since President Trump took office, consumer confidence has shown a sharp partisan split, with Republicans feeling far better about the economy than Democrats. This month's midterm elections, in which Democrats retook control of the House of Representatives, may have begun to narrow that gap.

SurveyMonkey took its survey the week of the election, conducting about 4,300 online interviews on or before Election Day and 5,000 after the results were known. Among Democrats and independents, the results changed little over the course of the survey.

But for Republicans, there was a clear shift in outlook: Among Republicans interviewed before the election, 66 percent said they expected their finances to improve over the next year. Among those interviewed afterward, that share fell to 59 percent. The effect was particularly pronounced among strong supporters of Mr. Trump, who showed a nine-point decline after the election in the share expecting their finances to be better a year from now.

BEN CASSELMAN writes about economics, with a particular focus on stories involving data. He previously reported for FiveThirtyEight and The Wall Street Journal.

CHAPTER 4

Consumer Behaviors

Every year, millions of dollars fund numerous studies devoted to understanding why people buy what they buy and what factors influence their decisions. Retailers study the findings of this research closely. To understand consumer behavior is to gain a big leg up in attracting and keeping customers. The articles in this chapter explore the patterns evident in consumer behavior and some of the psychology that undergirds it.

What People Buy Where

OPINION | BY ELIZABETH CURRID-HALKETT | DEC. 13, 2014

CONSPICUOUS CONSUMPTION IS everywhere, but it's not the same everywhere. People living in certain cities spend far more than the national average on particular goods and services that they believe will enhance their social standing.

In New York City, favored items include luxury watches and shoes. In Boston, the status signal of choice is tuition to a private school. Clothes are the go-to goods in Dallas. Wearing high-end makeup says you've arrived in Phoenix. In San Francisco, one telling sign is women's sport coats and tailored jackets. And in Washington, D.C., encyclopedias and reference books are top status markers. Go figure.

I study urban economies for a living and what I found made me wonder if the different profiles cities present to the world have as much to do with their consumption patterns as with their local industries. To find out, I used the Bureau of Labor Statistics' Consumer Expenditure Survey to track differences among cities in household spending from 2007 to 2012.

The survey dates to the 1800s but has only recently broken out detailed information on the spending habits, incomes and demographics of its respondents in the nation's metropolitan areas. With a collaborator, Hyojung Lee, a doctoral candidate in urban planning, I tracked differences in purchases of almost 1,000 items, from watches to loaves of bread — and even alimony. We divided this data into items that are conspicuously consumed, like cars, TVs, shoes and jewelry, and the more humdrum purchases of day-to-day life. Then we compared cities.

It will not shock you to learn that if you live in one of the five boroughs of New York City or in Los Angeles, you spend more money on conspicuous goods, on average (both in absolute terms and as a share of total expenditures), than you do if you live in Boston or Phoenix. But it is revealing that you do this whether you are rich or poor or somewhere in between.

The range of big spenders is also broader than you might expect. San Diego and Dallas outspend Boston and Phoenix on conspicuous consumption. The average household in Dallas will spend about 17 percent more — roughly $850 more per year — on status goods like watches, jewelry, high-end makeup and country-club memberships than a similar household in Boston.

Crucially, people in different metropolitan areas also buy significantly different items. The average household in the nation spends approximately $5,000 per year on conspicuous items, but that spending is expressed in varying ways. In 2012 in Dallas, curtains, draperies, decorative pillows, lamps and floor coverings accounted, in part, for above-average conspicuous spending. In Boston, it was fancy wine in restaurants and bars. And in Phoenix, residents spend above the national average on their pets.

In terms of pecking order, New Yorkers are tops when it comes to spending on status goods, followed by residents of Dallas, Los Angeles and San Diego. Even when we account for income, age and education levels, New Yorkers shell out 41 percent more — about $6,930 per year — than the national average. People who live in Boston, Phoenix and, perhaps surprisingly, Miami spend less on such goods.

Bostonians spend more on college and private-school tuition, give more money to political and charitable institutions and consume more coffee and books. In Miami and Phoenix, spending on education is significantly less than the national average, but Miami residents are above average in giving away their money to schools. They also devote an extraordinary amount of cash to parking spaces and car leases. Residents in Boston and Miami are above-average spenders on vacation homes.

Giving New York a run in the status sweepstakes is Dallas.

These two cities may be winning the conspicuous consumption race because of the type of people who live in and around New York or Dallas, but this "place effect" holds true no matter who you are, what you do or how much money you make. Just by virtue of living in a particular city, you tend to spend more or less on certain conspicuous items.

Some of these distinctive consumption habits reflect culture and priorities. Besides watches and shoes, New Yorkers devote far more of their money to limos, taxis and street-vendor breakfasts than the national average.

Sometimes they're just weird. People in San Diego spend 3.5 times more than everyone else on nonalcoholic beer. In San Francisco, alimony payments are the second biggest line item in total expenditures, 3.5 times the national average's share. Boston's most significant departure from the consumption norm is the rental of campers for out-of-town trips, 7.5 times the national average. The city, at 2.7 times the national average, also has an affection for dried peas.

Coined in the late 1800s by the economist Thorstein Veblen, the term "conspicuous consumption" primarily denoted the practices of what Veblen famously called "the leisure class," rich people with nothing better to do than to buy stuff to flaunt their wealth.

But consumption is not the exclusive hobby of the super wealthy. It transcends income, education and race. Place, meanwhile, not only influences how much of your income you spend on status goods. It also shapes your choices.

What's the best way to signal status in a city like New York, which lacks a definitive car culture? The luxury watch. New Yorkers spend about seven times the national average on watches. No other major metropolitan area in the country comes close. In 2010, when the city was slowly recovering from the financial meltdown of 2007 and 2008, New Yorkers still spent more than 25 times the national average on watches.

Women's clothes and shoes are another well-established marker of status, and people in New York and Dallas spend heavily accumulating them. New Yorkers spend 67 percent more on clothes, and 92 percent more on shoes, than the national average, while in Dallas, spending on clothes and shoes is 12 percent and 13 percent higher than average, respectively.

Our research also overturns some long-cherished city stereotypes. Today, despite the city's gilded reputation, the average New York resident is not into joining exclusive social clubs; he or she spends 17 percent less than the national average on such memberships. Forget San Francisco's fame as a city of bohemians and egalitarians; it leads the nation in spending on social, health and country-club memberships.

The biggest consumers of cosmetics and perfumes live in Los Angeles and New York, right? Not by a long shot. People in Phoenix, Houston, Minneapolis and Seattle spend 10 percent to 33 percent more than the national average catering to their physical appearance. But people in Boston and Baltimore have us all beat with their fondness for looking natural: They spend 25 percent less than the national average on superficiality.

One last reputation spoiler: Residents in the publishing capital are not avid readers. New Yorkers spend 28 percent less than the national average on books and 2 percent less on newspapers and magazines. Residents of Seattle and San Francisco are the most prolific consumers of books; they spend one and a half times the national average. Bostonians get the prize for most informed, forking over 40 percent more than the national average for newspapers and magazines.

Why are cities hotbeds of conspicuous consumption? There is no reason to believe that rural populations are less preoccupied with status, but cities are dense concentrations of people whose urban lifestyles make them — and their status — more visible to each other.

Measuring what appear to be relatively insignificant spending choices in cities may illuminate cultural, political and social differences.

If we self-select into certain cities and those cities then further influence and shape our priorities — or, for that matter, if a city's natives find themselves trying to keep up with the people moving in — we can expect increasing homogeneity within socio-geographical groups. This will not make us less polarized.

If this keeps up, a resident of Miami may be less likely to find the surroundings of Boston congenial. It will no longer just be about fear of the weather or a distaste for dried peas. The geography of conspicuous consumption shows us who we are and who we are becoming.

ELIZABETH CURRID-HALKETT is an associate professor at the University of Southern California's Price School of Public Policy and the author of "Starstruck: The Business of Celebrity."

Digital Culture, Meet Analog Fever

OPINION | BY ROB WALKER | NOV. 28, 2015

IN THE COURSE of a recent move, I decided to "cut the cord" — that is, walk away from cable television and fully embrace the streamed-entertainment revolution. I felt very digital. Just a few weeks later, however, I discovered something that surprised me: Thousands of my fellow cord-cutters have taken to buying antennas, to pick up the seemingly quaint format of over-the-air television signals.

I initially resisted joining those going out of their way to spend extra money on an object that was traditionally part of the default TV apparatus. But of course these are not your father's antennas, as they say: The new iteration promises far better picture quality over greater range, without constant adjustment (or strategic tinfoil enhancement).

Still, the return of the antenna struck me as not just retro, but counterrevolutionary. Could there be a more symbolic manifestation of the analog life than buying a contemporary version of rabbit ears? Soon I got an answer: Amazon, a company practically synonymous with the triumph of bits-in-the-cloud over objects-in-physical-space, just opened a brick-and-mortar bookstore.

Since then, I've been tuned in to evidence that our digital culture appears to have a case of analog fever. The rising sales of vinyl records, for instance, have been widely chronicled. E-book sales dropped by 10 percent in the first five months of this year, but Amazon's physical shop has plenty of company: The American Booksellers Association counted 1,712 member stores in 2015, up from 1,410 in 2010. You can't scroll through a lifestyle app without finding news of a precious new print journal's launch party; Etsy is thick with letterpress-printed offerings; and the digital-only publication Vox recently published an impassioned brief on behalf of the video rental store. The writer and artist David Rees hyped his TV show "Going Deep" by skipping

Twitter and Facebook in favor of putting up old-school promotional fliers — an "analog social media strategy," as he called it. And so on.

Just a couple of years ago bits seemed so unstoppable. Does the recent vogue for the physical suggest a decisive backlash — a regression in the direction of wax cylinders and stone tablets? It does not. What's going on instead is more interesting than that, or than mere nostalgia or even some strain of reactionary Luddism. It turns out that while the digital often comes close to crushing its analog precedents, that process can do something curious to its putative victims: underscore their virtues, elevate their status and transform the formerly workaday into something rarefied, special, even luxurious.

The relationship between the analog and the digital is more complicated than its usual portrayal. For starters, the pronouncement that some new technology X will "kill" some existing technology Y is usually just glib and easy hyperbole.

This was memorably demonstrated a couple of years ago, when the author Kevin Kelly asserted the opposite: "There is no species of technology that has ever gone globally extinct." In short: X *never* kills Y. That argument caught the attention of the journalist Robert Krulwich, who wondered: What about carbon paper, bronze helmets, chariot components? "Inventions, like dinosaurs, can go extinct," he insisted. Mr. Kelly stood firm; Mr. Krulwich's readers offered thousands of potential counterexamples. But everything from buggy whips to eight-track tapes turned out to be still in (however small) production. Arriving at a conclusive repudiation proved challenging enough that Mr. Krulwich graciously conceded the larger point that tools and technologies are shockingly difficult to kill off decisively.

Now take another look at, say, vinyl records, and it seems obvious that such a truly mass-consumed format would still be around. What's less obvious is that it would somehow transform into a fetish object. New LPs today are routinely advertised as being pressed on "180-gram vinyl," or some such. As someone who remembers vinyl's mass market heyday, when even stores like Sears had a record department,

I can assure you that nobody was agonizing over the physical specs of REO Speedwagon's "Hi Infidelity." But deposed as a mass good, the record has re-emerged as a de facto luxury good — a boutique version of its former self. What has really changed is not the intrinsic nature of analog objects or processes, but rather our attitude toward them.

After all, in terms of pure "democratization" — meaning, in this context, affordability, ubiquity and convenience — digital music really has trounced its analog precedents. Maybe it's the case, then, that deeper immersion in the digital is precisely what make us appreciate certain superior qualities of analog alternatives.

And yet, any argument that analog fever is a purely rational matter — old stuff is just plain better! — seems fishy. There's a murkier romance involved, a variation on the process that rebrands the dated as "vintage," "traditional" or "artisanal." The very marginalization of the analog has propelled it into the realm of luxury, by making its admirers come up with an answer to the obvious question: Why squander extra money and/or time on a less efficient alternative to the digital?

Consider the business card. Reasonable observers are constantly predicting its disappearance, or wondering why it persists. Obviously the swapping of contact particulars can be achieved without handing around objects (and, let's face it, transferring the information they convey into some more useful digital form). But that reality has upped the ante on business card creativity. A card that's made of concrete, doubles as a cheese grater, or can be reassembled into a toy — all of which exist — sends a message that's a lot more memorable than a Twitter handle. Even a letterpress card makes an impression no bits can match.

Is that about quality and intrinsic superiority? Or is it of a piece with the popular theory that practically all human decisions are mindless signals — of status, taste, distinction — directed at an audience of peers and strangers?

Our evolving relationship to the physical and the digital reveals another answer. When there is a bits-only version of almost anything, opting for the analog variation demonstrates what we *really* care about — to the world and to ourselves. To own or experience the analog version of the latest from a favorite musician, author, filmmaker and so on, is an act both sensual and symbolic.

And by now, that applies even to things that were never analog to begin with. The quiet phenomenon of "dedigitization" has demonstrated this, in the form of everything from physical emoji jewelry to pixelated-patterned throw pillows to the Giphoscope, which takes a burst of smartphone video and renders it, flipbook-style, as something that can be watched on a "device made of metal and wood, handcrafted in Italy with devotion."

O.K., maybe those are weird examples. But let's say you take video games seriously. If so, you are no doubt a supporter of the smart and beautiful printed journal Kill Screen, currently striving to further upgrade its physical manifestation through its second Kickstarter campaign.

That's a perfect manifestation, actually, of the way that analog fever functions not in opposition to digital dominance, but in concert with it. The fresh appreciation of the physical owes a great deal to the new age of bits. I know about David Rees's amusing "analog social media" tour only because I watched videos about it on YouTube.

Also, of course, the new generation of TV antennas that put analog fever on my radar provide better imagery because broadcasting itself is digital now. And when I decided to buy a physical antenna to bring the retro glories of the local news into my modern, cut-cord household, I did all my research online — poring over digital charts and maps matching my ZIP code to broadcast towers, and cross-referencing that data with product specs and reviews. I'm sure I could have bought the physical object that I settled on at a brick-and-mortar store near me. But who has time? I ordered it from Amazon instead.

ROB WALKER is a writer on design and technology whose advice column, "The Workologist," appears every other weekend in the Sunday Business section of The Times.

Credit Cards Encourage Extra Spending as the Cash Habit Fades Away

BY NELSON D. SCHWARTZ | MARCH 25, 2016

NINA FALCONE HAS given up on cash.

Whenever and wherever possible, even at the vending machines in her building in Chicago, the 25-year-old marketer uses her Southwest Airlines Rapid Rewards card to collect points she says she uses for plane tickets to visit her family in California.

Ms. Falcone carefully follows the advice from consumer advocates and does not carry a balance from month to month or pay humongous interest charges.

But she admits there are probably some downsides to the ease of purchasing. Time magazines piled up around her apartment and gathered dust after she bought a subscription simply because it came with an offer for extra points. And she has increased the amount of time she spends shopping on the Internet because merchants offer incentives online for cardholders that are not available in stores.

"I haven't paid for a trip on Southwest in years," says Ms. Falcone, which may be technically true, but a host of economic and social science research suggests that consumers tend to spend more using plastic than they ever would with actual cash.

Incentives like frequent-flier miles or rewards points only amplify a temptation that banks and financial services companies have been profiting from for decades.

"When you vary the payment method, people are willing to pay more," said Duncan Simester, a professor of marketing at M.I.T. who published a landmark paper on the subject in 2001. "You're not forking over a dollar bill, so there is less sensation of loss."

With M.B.A. students as the subjects, Mr. Simester and a colleague, Drazen Prelec, held an auction of tickets to basketball and baseball games featuring two local teams, the Boston Celtics and the Boston Red Sox.

Some participants were told they would have to pay by credit card, others were informed that only cash would be accepted.

When credit cards were an option, the M.B.A. students offered to pay roughly twice as much as they were willing to hand over in cash for the same tickets.

"The most surprising thing was the size of the effect," said Mr. Simester, who titled the resulting paper 'Always Leave Home Without It: A Further Investigation of the Credit-Card Effect on Willingness to Pay.' "

He added that while it was not unusual to see spending patterns shift by 5 or 10 percent in experiments, "you don't see too many examples where people offer double what they would have otherwise."

But the ease of buying with plastic, or what marketers call "friction-free spending," is only half the story. Social scientists have also found that consumers have been conditioned by even the sight of credit card logos to want to spend more.

Unlike Mr. Simester, who created an experiment from scratch, Richard Feinberg of Purdue University persuaded restaurants near campus in West Lafayette, Ind., to let him study actual patrons' spending habits.

Mr. Feinberg placed credit card logos and symbols on some tables and left others without them, as normal. The sight of images associated with credit cards prompted diners to spend more and leave bigger tips.

A similar exercise in a faculty member's office produced larger donations to the United Way, Mr. Feinberg added, while credit card images bolstered sales at a Fannie May candy store.

"People spend more when these stimuli are present," he said. "Just as Pavlov found that dogs would salivate when they heard tones that were associated with food, people have been conditioned to associate credit cards with spending."

Although tools like Apple Pay and other mobile payment methods are too new to have generated much academic research, or allowed the kind of conditioning that half a century of credit card use has produced, Mr. Feinberg suggests a similar dynamic could be at work.

"The less friction there is, the easier it becomes to spend," he said. "Just stand at Starbucks and watch how many people there use their smartphones to buy a latte."

Speaking of lattes, credit cards also encourage people to pay more for everyday items than they might otherwise, according to Scott Bilker, founder of debtsmart.com and the author of "Talk Your Way Out of Credit Card Debt."

"Paying $5 for a coffee might seem like a lot if you only have $10 in your wallet," he said. "But if your credit card has a $10,000 limit on it, it doesn't seem like much."

The key, said Greg McBride, chief financial analyst at Bankrate. com, a personal finance website, is to try to exercise the same discipline with plastic that you would with cash, despite the urge to splurge.

If you can't help yourself, or occasionally do have to carry a balance, avoid incentive cards at all costs. "They only work for consumers who pay their balances in full," he said, as Ms. Falcone does scrupulously each month.

For the 60 percent of consumers who can't pay off what they owe each month, a much smarter bet would be to seek out the card with the lowest possible interest rate.

Of course, even the best card rates are still high — the typical consumer today has $2,200 in credit card debt, with an average annual interest rate of nearly 16 percent, according to Bankrate.com.

Does that mean consumers should cut their cards up, stick to cash the way our great-grandparents had to and embrace the supposedly traditional value of thrift?

It's not that simple today, nor was there really ever a golden age when Americans bought only what they could truly afford, said Lendol Calder, a professor of history at Augustana College in Rock Island, Ill.

"The river of red ink has run through American history from the beginning," said Mr. Calder. "The Pilgrims took out loans from London investors and many of them died without ever having paid off their debts. As far back as you go, people were in over their heads."

That said, Mr. Calder says he believes credit cards do offer advantages, despite the inevitable temptation to spend more.

"Credit cards are useful because people want to be thrifty with time," Mr. Calder explained. "In the 20th century, time became scarce and credit cards and credit in general helps with that. It's one thing to save and save and buy an engagement ring for someone you love, but not if you wait and she runs off with someone else."

NELSON D. SCHWARTZ is a reporter for The New York Times who covers the economy.

Paying With Cash Hurts.
That's Also Why It Feels So Good.

BY PHYLLIS KORKKI | JULY 16, 2016

PAYING WITH CASH is painful — and that's a good thing, according to new research.

When people pay for items using cold, hard cash rather than by card or online, they feel more of a sting and therefore assign more value to the purchase, according to Avni M. Shah, an assistant marketing professor at the University of Toronto Scarborough. Her findings were born of personal experience: One day she forgot her debit card, so she paid for a latte with physical dollars — and felt her drink tasted better that day. Could her method of payment have been the reason?

She tested her theory two years ago, when she was a doctoral student at Duke University. She decided to sell discounted mugs with the Duke University logo on them to school staff and faculty in their offices. She asked one group to pay $2 for the mugs with cash. The other group had to pay with a card.

Then Professor Shah returned to each purchaser two hours later and said she needed to buy the mug back. To soften the blow, she asked the buyers to name their price. The people who had paid for the mug with a card asked for an average of $3.83 back, while those who had paid with cash asked, on average, for $6.71.

"Some of the cash folks literally blocked their hand over the mug and said, 'You can't take this back,' " Professor Shah said.

Professor Shah, who also teaches at the Rotman School of Management, published her study in The Journal of Consumer Research. Her co-authors are Noah Eisenkraft, James R. Bettman and Tanya L. Chartrand.

In another study, Professor Shah gave $5 to her research participants to donate to one of three causes. One group received the amount in cash, and the other in the form of a voucher. Then she gave the participants a ribbon that they could wear on their lapels to show that they had made a donation.

Later, about half the people who had made the donation with cash reported wearing the ribbon, whereas only 14 percent of the voucher group had done so. It suggested that the cash group — and it hadn't even been their cash — felt more of an emotional connection to the cause.

Of all the payment methods, "Cash feels the most painful," Professor Shah said. "Even a check feels quite painful." Therefore the purchase is more meaningful. In a separate study involving charitable donations, she found that people who donated by check were more likely to make a repeat donation the next year compared with those who had donated by card.

Card and digital payments seem less real than cash, she said. It's true that the unreality of these methods can cause people to make more purchases in the first place (to the detriment of their finances). But those same people tend to be less loyal to particular brands, Professor Shah said. "It's an 'out with the old, in with the new' mentality."

"I'm not saying we should revert back to cash," she added. But there are ways to make the fact that people are parting with their money more vivid, she said — for example by introducing a buzzing noise into the process or sending an email reminder of the transaction.

If companies and organizations want to encourage repeat business, they may want to return a little more pain to the payment process, she said.

Consumers May Be More Trusting of Ads Than Marketers Think

BY ZACH SCHONBRUN | JULY 30, 2017

THE EARLY RESULTS from a recent study that Kent Grayson, a Northwestern University marketing professor, did on consumer skepticism left him feeling a little, well, skeptical.

So he ran the trials a few more times. Each time, when participants were asked what they thought of modern advertising techniques, they answered with words like "credible," "fair" and "good."

The study, done by Mr. Grayson and Mathew Isaac, a professor at Seattle University, and published in April in the Journal of Consumer Research, surveyed 400 participants regarding 20 common tactics used in television and digital ads. Thirteen of the tactics elicited favorable responses, which surprised even marketers.

"Right off the bat, I was wondering, 'Who did they talk to?' " said James Shani, founder and chief executive of Madison & Vine, a digital studio in Los Angeles.

It is no secret that advertisers have faced difficulty getting through to savvier audiences that are far less trusting of brands and institutions than previous generations. Indeed, that notion formed the basis of what Mr. Grayson intended to examine when he began his research last year.

"Our hypothesis was that maybe it's more nuanced than that," Mr. Grayson said. "People have said, 'I don't trust advertising.' The truth is, there is a lot of advertising that they do trust."

Certain tactics, such as offering to match a competitor's low prices, reporting a high rating on a site like Amazon or Yelp or mentioning a recent ranking by a third-party source like U.S. News & World Report, received the most positive reactions from participants. Others, like using paid actors instead of real people, or even hiring celebrity endorsers to express their affinity for a product, came off as "deceptive" or "manipulative," according to those surveyed.

Jake Sorofman, who analyzes marketing trends as a vice president and chief of research for Gartner for Marketers, a research and consulting firm, said brands should already be recognizing that the "persuasion by way of manipulation" approaches of the past were not going to work on modern consumers.

"Consumers are certainly becoming more savvy, more skeptical, more discriminating," Mr. Sorofman said. "They expect a lot more, and that's putting pressure on marketers to do better."

Chris Raih's conclusion is that consumers are willing to play along, as long as brands play fairly. Mr. Raih, the founder and president of Zambezi, a Los Angeles ad agency, wrote an essay for AdWeek in January about combating the "atmosphere of disbelief" that he felt had pervaded society. He argued that brands needed to better use their platforms to bridge gaps, communicate and inspire.

"We do see more nuance than what is reported," Mr. Raih wrote in an email. "Look, today's audience is more sophisticated than ever before. They know how the machine works. They know why Facebook ads retarget them based on previous searches. They know why brands buy space on certain programming. The mystique is gone."

Though the study demonstrated that all approaches are not equally unscrupulous in the eyes of consumers, some advertisers are trying to look beyond antiquated tactics for better ways to engage with people.

"We're advising our clients on the importance of 'proving' over 'selling' brand values," Adam Tucker, president of Ogilvy & Mather New York, wrote in an email. "Across the industry, we're seeing brands evolve their marketing communications to be more engaging, more participatory and, ultimately, more personalized."

Mr. Shani said the study reaffirmed his contention that people were looking foremost for authenticity from companies. Establishing that takes time; he compared it to putting money into an individual retirement account, where the dividends do not pay off for years.

"Authenticity is not a metric," Mr. Shani said. "It's the feeling you always get when you see a brand."

The researchers did not distinguish between age groups. Nor did they break down the tactics by presentation — print, digital or television — choosing to keep the formatting ambiguous.

"There's a lot of marketers out there that are trying to trick people," Mr. Grayson said. "They're willing to cheat consumers on the edges, such as by keeping the price the same but decreasing the food that's in the package by imperceptible amounts. We do have to go around with a certain amount of vigilance."

An important point, Mr. Isaac said, is that consumer disbelief about certain tactics can also be fluid. Some approaches deemed disreputable a few years ago could become more widely accepted. Product placements and native advertising — packaged to look like journalism — are two examples.

"I think the jury's out," Mr. Sorofman said, referring to native ads as manipulative. "But the best practices tend to ensure there's transparency. As long as there is transparency in the intent."

Asked what he felt about the "atmosphere of disbelief," Mr. Shani said he still wanted to double-check the researchers' work. "Did he mean credible or not credible?" Mr. Shani joked.

But the researchers hope that advertisers can embrace some bit of good news and home in on what they have demonstrated can work.

"I think there's a lot of bias out there that marketers already think they're behind the 8-ball a little bit, where consumers already think we're out to get them," Mr. Isaac said. "And that may not be the case. They might actually be starting from a greater position of strength than they think."

Apple's Biggest Problem? My Mom

COLUMN | BY KEVIN ROOSE | JAN. 5, 2019

WHEN APPLE LOST more than $75 billion in market value this past week after a surprise announcement that it is expecting lower iPhone sales than originally projected, the company put most of the blame for its troubles on China, where a slowing economy and the trade war with the United States have hurt sales.

But a bigger issue for Apple might exist much closer to home, in a small, leafy town in Ohio.

That's where my mom lives. She's a relatively tech-savvy retiree and a longtime Apple fan who has used many of the company's products over the years. I learned to type on an Apple IIGS at her office, and she was an early adopter of the original turquoise iMac. These days, she uses her iPhone to check Facebook and Instagram, talk with her friends and relatives, and play solitaire and Words With Friends.

Her phone isn't the latest model — it's a three-year-old iPhone 6S — and it's missing some of the latest features. She can't take portrait mode photos using a dual-lens camera, a feature introduced in the iPhone 7 Plus, and she can't unlock her phone using Face ID, which was introduced in the iPhone X in 2017. Her phone's battery life could be better, and the device sometimes runs out of storage space.

But she's happy with it, and doesn't feel the need to upgrade. She also has a first-generation Apple Watch and a several-versions-ago MacBook Air, neither of which she's planning to replace anytime soon.

"The phone I have does just about everything I need," she said when I called her to ask why she hadn't upgraded to one of the newer models. "Why pay $800 for a new one just to be up to date? My needs aren't that complicated."

Most of the journalists who write about tech for a living (including me) are early adopters — power users who like having the latest gadgets, and who are willing to fork over money for a slightly better experience. For some of these people, Apple's announcement has come as a shock that portends potential disaster for the company.

But for my mom, and the many people who are probably in her situation, the company's slowing iPhone sales aren't at all a disaster. In fact, they make total sense, and they don't have much to do with China.

In a letter to investors explaining the lower forecast, Timothy D. Cook, Apple's chief executive, nodded to smaller-than-expected demand for iPhone upgrades, saying that consumers were "adapting to a world with fewer carrier subsidies" and "taking advantage of significantly reduced pricing for iPhone battery replacements." The company declined to comment for this column.

Apple is also facing competition from rivals like Samsung and Huawei, which have flooded international markets with lower-cost Androids that are, in many cases, just as functional as iPhones. And, yes, there are issues related to President Trump's trade war with China, and an overall economic slowdown in the country.

But the most consequential hit to Apple's bottom line may be from people who are holding on to their phones for longer. Back in 2015, iPhones were being replaced after roughly two years, on average, according to BayStreet Research, a firm that tracks smartphone sales. That period has jumped to roughly three years, and is expected to grow even more.

"We're going to move to longer replacement cycles, principally because the cost is higher," said Chris Caso, a tech analyst with Raymond James.

Many of Apple's issues are common to smartphone makers. The components inside newer phones, such as added memory and improved screen technology, are more expensive than older components. Refurbished and used phones are also more easily available, and carriers like Verizon and AT&T aren't subsidizing new phone purchases as heavily as they once did, meaning that the up-front cost to the customer is higher.

An Apple store in Beijing. With new iPhones costing more than ever, "we're going to move to longer replacement cycles," said Chris Caso, a tech analyst with Raymond James.

"It used to be that for $650, you got all new features, a better screen, everything," Mr. Caso said. "Now, to put more features in the phone, it costs money."

There are Apple-specific variables, too. The newest version of Apple's mobile operating systems, iOS 12, was designed to improve the performance of older devices. (This was a refreshing change from previous iOS updates, which tended to grind older models to a halt.) With better water resistance and sturdier screens, iPhones are more physically resilient than they used to be. And the list of must-have new features has shrunk. With a few exceptions — like Face ID and animated emojis — there is nothing you can do on a new iPhone that you can't do on one from several years ago.

Apple has also taken a hit from its battery replacement program, which offered steep discounts to many customers after the company was accused of slowing down older iPhones. That led some users to replace their batteries rather than their entire iPhone.

All of this is worrying short-term investors, who want people to buy as many new iPhones as possible. But it's great for people like my mom, who get to keep phones they're happy with and replace them less frequently. It's great for the environment — according to Apple's latest sustainability report, each new Apple device produced generates an average of 90 kilograms of carbon emissions.

A more durable iPhone could even be great for Apple's long-term profitability. As Brian Barrett points out at Wired, "An iPhone that lasts longer keeps customers in the iOS ecosystem longer," and more willing to keep their paid subscriptions to Apple Music, iCloud and other Apple services.

Apple's longer replacement cycle may be a temporary phenomenon, if newer technologies — such as compatibility with 5G mobile networks, which is expected to arrive in iPhones in 2020 — lead to popular apps that don't run on older phones.

"If there's an app — maybe it's Fortnite 2 — that I can't run on my existing iPhone, a new iPhone will be on every teenage boy's shopping list," Mr. Caso said.

But for now, while investors might be unhappy with the company's short-term sales, the rest of us should cheer it as a sign of progress in giving customers what they want: sturdy, reliable phones that don't become obsolete as soon as a new model arrives.

When I asked my mom what would get her to upgrade to a newer iPhone, she said she might do it if a new, killer feature came along, or if her favorite apps no longer worked. But in the end, she admitted that wasn't likely.

"Until I drop it and break it, I'll probably keep it," she said.

KEVIN ROOSE is a columnist for Business Day and a writer-at-large for The New York Times Magazine. His column, "The Shift," examines the intersection of technology, business and culture.

CHAPTER 5

Critiquing Consumerism

Even as consumerism has become inextricable from mainstream American life, it has not done so without attracting its fair share of criticism. Commentators and economists point to the dehumanizing consequences of consumer culture, as well as the larger power structures individual consumerism enforces. The articles in this section present a variety of critiques of consumer culture from economic, social and political perspectives.

Preaching to Save Shoppers From 'Evil' of Consumerism

BY CONSTANCE L. HAYS | JAN. 1, 2003

SOME PEOPLE MAY BE UPSET that retail sales failed to meet expectations during the holiday season. Not Bill Talen.

For the last four years Mr. Talen, also known as Reverend Billy, has been performing from the theaters of Bleecker Street to the Starbucks on Astor Place, exhorting people to resist temptation — the temptation to shop — and to smite the demon of consumerism.

With the zeal of a street-corner preacher and the schmaltz of a street-corner Santa, Reverend Billy, 52, will tell anyone willing to listen that people are walking willingly into the hellfires of consumption.

Shoppers have little regard for how or where or by whom the products they buy are made, he believes. They have almost no resistance to the media messages that encourage them, around the clock, to want things and buy them. He sees a population lost in consumption, the meaning of individual existence vanished in a fog of wanting, buying and owning too many things.

"Consumerism is a dull way of life," he says. "We're all sinners. We're all shoppers. Let's do what we can."

It's an act, a kind of performance art, almost a form of religion. He named it the Church of Stop Shopping. As Reverend Billy, he wears a televangelist's pompadour and a priest's collar, and is often accompanied by his gospel choir when he strides into stores he considers objectionable or shows up at protests like the annual post-Thanksgiving Buy Nothing Day event on Fifth Avenue in Manhattan.

The choir, which is made up of volunteers, includes people like David Glover and his daughter, Zena, from Brooklyn. There is also Beka Economopoulos, who once sang at the White House, and Meredith Manna, who came in courtesy of one of the keyboard players. When they erupt in song, it is hard to ignore: "Stop shopping! Stop shopping! We will never shop again!"

Other performers preach the same gospel, with their own twists. Ange Taggart, who lives in Nottingham, England, turns up in places like Troy, N.Y., to go into a store, buy a lot of things, and then return them. She recently filled a cart with Martha Stewart products at Kmart, then put them on the conveyor in a certain order, so that when she got her receipt, she said, the first letters on the itemized list spelled "Martha Stewart's hell."

There is also Andrew Lynn, who created Whirl-Mart last year. He gets a group of people together, everyone with a shopping cart, and they stroll the aisles of Wal-Mart or Kmart, putting nothing in the carts. When store managers tell him to take his protest elsewhere, he tells them: "This isn't a protest. We're performing a consumption-awareness ritual."

There may be something to it, too. Psychologists at the University of Rochester and at Knox College in Illinois have published studies concluding that people focused on "extrinsic" goals like money are more depressed than others and report more behavioral problems and physical discomfort.

Some economists have also addressed the phenomenon of rich people who feel poor. Juliet B. Schor of Harvard University, the author of "The Overspent American" (Basic Books, 1998), says people are frustrated because they compare their lives with what they see on television. Robert H. Frank of Cornell reached a similar conclusion in "Luxury Fever: Why Money Fails to Satisfy in an Era of Excess" (The Free Press, 1999).

It's not that Reverend Billy thinks no one should ever buy anything; on a recent afternoon, he himself was seen purchasing a ream of printer paper and a bottle of wine. It is the futility of shopping he is trying to address — the futility of leaning too heavily on the material at the expense of the spiritual and emotional.

That mission has given focus to his art, his politics and even his religion. Raised by what he calls "strict Dutch Calvinists" in Rochester, Minn., he made his way to New York in the early 1990's. He had his epiphany in 1999, when protesters disrupted the World Trade Organization meetings in Seattle; he discovered the potential of drama to send a political message.

He discussed the revelation with a friend, Sidney Lanier, an Episcopal minister and cousin of Tennessee Williams who had used theater to evoke social reform themes in the 1960's. Mr. Talen soon realized that after years of producing Spalding Gray and others, he suddenly had an act of his own.

Mr. Lanier said he suggested a man of the cloth as a vehicle for Mr. Talen's message. "I encouraged him," he said. "I said, you have a kind of Calvinist preacher in you that wants to come out."

Mr. Talen, even before he developed the character, said he admired the cadence and the poetry of good fire and brimstone. Child labor, environmental damage and evidence of union busting by big retail chains, all to deliver low prices to consumers, provided plenty of material for any pulpit. "I sense right now that our lives are getting absurd," he said.

On a recent evangelical side trip, Mr. Talen ventured into the Kmart on Astor Place, where speakers blared Elvis and Tom Petty Christmas carols. His own face blank, he began to look for smiley-faces, which he considers one of the most nefarious of marketing tools. He found them on signs, on children's pajamas, on stickers. Few of the shoppers, however, were smiling, he noticed. And that is part of the problem.

"The smile has been so thoroughly appropriated by transnational capital," he said. "They discovered that smiling makes money."

When he left Kmart, he walked down Lafayette Street, bellowing now and then in character about how creeping consumerism threatens the fabric of society, in the form of chain stores, sweatshops and more.

But to the public, it mostly just means more stuff to buy at a good price. Indeed, it is no surprise that Reverend Billy has not had much of an impact. Even this year, considered to be a particularly disappointing Christmas shopping season, Americans are still expected to spend almost $1 trillion at stores, restaurants and auto dealers in the last three months of 2002, up perhaps 3 to 4 percent from the year before.

"They don't care!" Reverend Billy shouted to no one in particular on a dark stretch of Lafayette Street, as people carrying shopping bags from J. Crew, Macy's and the Gap poured into a nearby subway entrance.

"They do care," a bearded man beside a scaffolding replied. "They just have a bad attitude."

"Hallelujah!" Reverend Billy said. He says that a lot.

The Reverend Billy made his first formal appearance at the Disney store in Times Square, circa 1998. He was driven away in a police car, his wrists still cuffed to a large statue of Mickey Mouse. The store has since closed.

He has found other targets; in general, he selects large global companies that he feels are inappropriately seizing control. In 1999, he zeroed in on Starbucks. He was pleased to discover later that he had become the subject of a company memo.

"Reverend Billy sits quietly at a table with devotees and then begins to chat up the customers," the memo, dated April 24, 2000, reads. "He works the crowd with an affirming theme but gradually turns on Starbucks. Toward the end, he's shouting." And it adds: "According to a store manager, he may stand on your tables."

Audrey Lincuff, a Starbucks spokeswoman, confirmed the authenticity of the memo — and disputed the accuracy of Reverend Billy's message, at least as it pertains to Starbucks. "We consider ourselves to be locally relevant where we do business," she said, "and work very hard to weave ourselves into the fabric of the community by associating and working with nonprofit groups and other community groups." The company's goal, she added, is to "connect with our customers not only on a business level but on things that are important to them in their lives."

Reverend Billy says he tries to remain relatively low key. "I'm against a lot of political people who have become fundamentalists themselves," he said. He doesn't like the anti-fur people who ridicule pedestrians in fur coats or hats, for example. He is a latte drinker, though he doesn't order it at Starbucks.

He wants to help awaken desensitized shoppers, he says, because "they are underestimating the complexity and beauty of life." And besides, "they are definitely underestimating the impact of shopping."

Americans as Addicts of Consumerism

REVIEW | BY ED BARK | APRIL 12, 2008

WHAT PIGS WE ARE.

Or to put it even more directly, the "average American" consumes 1.7 tons of pork in a lifetime, according to one of the myriad facts and figures in "Human Footprint" on the National Geographic Channel.

This two-hour production, having its premiere on Sunday, with Elizabeth Vargas of ABC News as anchor, is never more than a commercial break away from another armload of weighty statistics.

Many are painstakingly illustrated by the average lifelong mass quantities of diapers (3,796), pints of milk (13,056), bananas (5,067), beers (13,248) and so on. In some cases a little product placement goes a long way, as when a prominent bread maker's logo can be seen on a grand total of 4,376 loaves.

Later the filmmakers imaginatively use 28,443 yellow rubber duckies to dramatize a lifetime's worth of showers at the expense of 700,000 gallons of water.

No special effects were used for any of these displays, National Geographic says. The signature overhead shot, in all its glory, is of 12,129 hamburger buns and 5,442 hot dog rolls arranged in the shape of the American flag. Be still, my thumping heart. But where's the apple pie?

The statistics were compiled in partnership with the Wildlife Conservation Society, based at the Bronx Zoo, and the Earth Institute at Columbia University. They're based on a life expectancy of 77 years 9 months, and a United States population rounded to 301 million. "Human Footprint" tracks supposedly typical consumers from diaper-wearing infancy to medication-dependent old age.

Not surprisingly, Americans continue to out-big-foot everyone else when it comes to consumption. Although only 5 percent of the global population, Americans are said to use more than one-quarter of the world's energy.

Ms. Vargas dutifully spews out the stats like an old-school adding machine. But it all gets more than a little wearying, once the wow factor has receded. All right, all right, enough with the prolonged shower of a lifetime's worth of 19,826 eggs sent splattering into an unsightly "omelet of a lifetime," as she says.

The script is serviceable although at times a bit hackneyed.

"As much as we relish our hot dogs, that's nothing compared to our love affair with the hamburger," Ms. Vargas says at one point. She adds, "It's an ugly fact that Americans spend more on beauty than on education every year."

The review copy of "Human Footprint" is notably skimpy on what exactly to do about all of this — or how harmful it might be. National Geographic's program materials say the final cut will incorporate public service spots and "Web pointers" with "suggestions for reducing your human footprint" and its attendant carbon dioxide emissions. Ms. Vargas, for her part, tells viewers that it would be a good idea to lower thermostats, use new energy-saving light bulbs and unplug appliances when not in use.

Parochially speaking, it might be good to keep one consumptive statistic in mind. "Human Footprint" says that each lifetime reader of The New York Times uses 40,040 pounds of newsprint.

Read into that what you will, but let's not get carried away with any crazy starvation diets.

HUMAN FOOTPRINT

National Geographic, Sunday night at 9, Eastern and Pacific times; 8, Central time.

Malcolm Brinkworth, executive producer for Touch Productions; Clive Maltby, producer, director and writer; Produced by Touch Productions for the National Geographic Channel; Howard Swartz, executive producer for the National Geographic Channel.

WITH: Elizabeth Vargas.

But Will It Make You Happy?

BY **STEPHANIE ROSENBLOOM** | AUG. 7, 2010

SHE HAD SO MUCH.

A two-bedroom apartment. Two cars. Enough wedding china to serve two dozen people.

Yet Tammy Strobel wasn't happy. Working as a project manager with an investment management firm in Davis, Calif., and making about $40,000 a year, she was, as she put it, caught in the "work-spend treadmill."

So one day she stepped off.

Inspired by books and blog entries about living simply, Ms. Strobel and her husband, Logan Smith, both 31, began donating some of their belongings to charity. As the months passed, out went stacks of sweaters, shoes, books, pots and pans, even the television after a trial separation during which it was relegated to a closet. Eventually, they got rid of their cars, too. Emboldened by a Web site that challenges consumers to live with just 100 personal items, Ms. Strobel winnowed down her wardrobe and toiletries to precisely that number.

Her mother called her crazy.

Today, three years after Ms. Strobel and Mr. Smith began downsizing, they live in Portland, Ore., in a spare, 400-square-foot studio with a nice-sized kitchen. Mr. Smith is completing a doctorate in physiology; Ms. Strobel happily works from home as a Web designer and freelance writer. She owns four plates, three pairs of shoes and two pots. With Mr. Smith in his final weeks of school, Ms. Strobel's income of about $24,000 a year covers their bills. They are still car-free but have bikes. One other thing they no longer have: $30,000 of debt.

Ms. Strobel's mother is impressed. Now the couple have money to travel and to contribute to the education funds of nieces and nephews. And because their debt is paid off, Ms. Strobel works fewer hours, giving her time to be outdoors, and to volunteer, which she does about four hours a week for a nonprofit outreach program called Living Yoga.

"The idea that you need to go bigger to be happy is false," she says. "I really believe that the acquisition of material goods doesn't bring about happiness."

While Ms. Strobel and her husband overhauled their spending habits before the recession, legions of other consumers have since had to reconsider their own lifestyles, bringing a major shift in the nation's consumption patterns.

"We're moving from a conspicuous consumption — which is 'buy without regard' — to a calculated consumption," says Marshal Cohen, an analyst at the NPD Group, the retailing research and consulting firm.

Amid weak job and housing markets, consumers are saving more and spending less than they have in decades, and industry professionals expect that trend to continue. Consumers saved 6.4 percent of their after-tax income in June, according to a new government report. Before the recession, the rate was 1 to 2 percent for many years. In June, consumer spending and personal incomes were essentially flat compared with May, suggesting that the American economy, as dependent as it is on shoppers opening their wallets and purses, isn't likely to rebound anytime soon.

On the bright side, the practices that consumers have adopted in response to the economic crisis ultimately could — as a raft of new research suggests — make them happier. New studies of consumption and happiness show, for instance, that people are happier when they spend money on experiences instead of material objects, when they relish what they plan to buy long before they buy it, and when they stop trying to outdo the Joneses.

If consumers end up sticking with their newfound spending habits, some tactics that retailers and marketers began deploying during the recession could become lasting business strategies. Among those strategies are proffering merchandise that makes being at home more

Tammy Strobel and her husband, Logan Smith, in their pared-down, 400-square-foot apartment in Portland, Ore.

entertaining and trying to make consumers feel special by giving them access to exclusive events and more personal customer service.

While the current round of stinginess may simply be a response to the economic downturn, some analysts say consumers may also be permanently adjusting their spending based on what they've discovered about what truly makes them happy or fulfilled.

"This actually is a topic that hasn't been researched very much until recently," says Elizabeth W. Dunn, an associate professor in the psychology department at the University of British Columbia, who is at the forefront of research on consumption and happiness. "There's massive literature on income and happiness. It's amazing how little there is on how to spend your money."

Conspicuous consumption has been an object of fascination going back at least as far as 1899, when the economist Thorstein Veblen published "The Theory of the Leisure Class," a book that analyzed, in part, how people spent their money in order to demonstrate their social status.

And it's been a truism for eons that extra cash always makes life a little easier. Studies over the last few decades have shown that money, up to a certain point, makes people happier because it lets them meet basic needs. The latest round of research is, for lack of a better term, all about emotional efficiency: how to reap the most happiness for your dollar.

So just where does happiness reside for consumers? Scholars and researchers haven't determined whether Armani will put a bigger smile on your face than Dolce & Gabbana. But they have found that our types of purchases, their size and frequency, and even the timing of the spending all affect long-term happiness.

One major finding is that spending money for an experience — concert tickets, French lessons, sushi-rolling classes, a hotel room in Monaco — produces longer-lasting satisfaction than spending money on plain old stuff.

" 'It's better to go on a vacation than buy a new couch' is basically the idea," says Professor Dunn, summing up research by two fellow psychologists, Leaf Van Boven and Thomas Gilovich. Her own take on the subject is in a paper she wrote with colleagues at Harvard and the University of Virginia: "If Money Doesn't Make You Happy Then You Probably Aren't Spending It Right." (The Journal of Consumer Psychology plans to publish it in a coming issue.)

Thomas DeLeire, an associate professor of public affairs, population, health and economics at the University of Wisconsin in Madison, recently published research examining nine major categories of consumption. He and Ariel Kalil of the University of Chicago discovered that the only category to be positively related to happiness was leisure: vacations, entertainment, sports and equipment like golf clubs and fishing poles.

Using data from a study by the National Institute on Aging, Professor DeLeire compared the happiness derived from different levels

VIKTOR KOEN

of spending to the happiness people get from being married. (Studies have shown that marriage increases happiness.)

"A $20,000 increase in spending on leisure was roughly equivalent to the happiness boost one gets from marriage," he said, adding that spending on leisure activities appeared to make people less lonely and increased their interactions with others.

According to retailers and analysts, consumers have gravitated more toward experiences than possessions over the last couple of years, opting to use their extra cash for nights at home with family, watching movies and playing games — or for "staycations" in the backyard. Many retailing professionals think this is not a fad, but rather "the new normal."

"I think many of these changes are permanent changes," says Jennifer Black, president of the retailing research company Jennifer Black & Associates and a member of the Governor's Council of Economic Advisors in Oregon. "I think people are realizing they don't need what they had. They're more interested in creating memories."

She largely attributes this to baby boomers' continuing concerns about the job market and their ability to send their children to college. While they will still spend, they will spend less, she said, having reset their priorities.

While it is unlikely that most consumers will downsize as much as Ms. Strobel did, many have been, well, happily surprised by the pleasures of living a little more simply. The Boston Consulting Group said in a June report that recession anxiety had prompted a "back-to-basics movement," with things like home and family increasing in importance over the last two years, while things like luxury and status have declined.

"There's been an emotional rebirth connected to acquiring things that's really come out of this recession," says Wendy Liebmann, chief executive of WSL Strategic Retail, a marketing consulting firm that works with manufacturers and retailers. "We hear people talking about the desire not to lose that — that connection, the moment, the family, the experience."

Current research suggests that, unlike consumption of material goods, spending on leisure and services typically strengthens social bonds, which in turn helps amplify happiness. (Academics are already in broad agreement that there is a strong correlation between the quality of people's relationships and their happiness; hence, anything that promotes stronger social bonds has a good chance of making us feel all warm and fuzzy.)

And the creation of complex, sophisticated relationships is a rare thing in the world. As Professor Dunn and her colleagues Daniel T. Gilbert and Timothy D. Wilson point out in their forthcoming paper, only termites, naked mole rats and certain insects like ants and bees construct social networks as complex as those of human beings. In that elite little club, humans are the only ones who shop.

At the height of the recession in 2008, Wal-Mart Stores realized that consumers were "cocooning" — vacationing in their yards, eating more dinners at home, organizing family game nights. So it responded by grouping items in its stores that would turn any den into an at-home movie theater or transform a backyard into a slice of the Catskills. Wal-Mart wasn't just selling barbecues and board games. It was selling experiences.

"We spend a lot of time listening to our customers," says Amy Lester, a spokeswoman for Wal-Mart, "and know that they have a set amount to spend and need to juggle to meet that amount."

One reason that paying for experiences gives us longer-lasting happiness is that we can reminisce about them, researchers say. That's true for even the most middling of experiences. That trip to Rome during which you waited in endless lines, broke your camera and argued with your spouse will typically be airbrushed with "rosy recollection," says Sonja Lyubomirsky, a psychology professor at the University of California, Riverside.

Professor Lyubomirsky has a grant from the National Institute of Mental Health to conduct research on the possibility of permanently increasing happiness. "Trips aren't all perfect," she notes, "but we remember them as perfect."

Another reason that scholars contend that experiences provide a bigger pop than things is that they can't be absorbed in one gulp — it takes more time to adapt to them and engage with them than it does to put on a new leather jacket or turn on that shiny flat-screen TV.

"We buy a new house, we get accustomed to it," says Professor Lyubomirsky, who studies what psychologists call "hedonic adaptation," a phenomenon in which people quickly become used to changes, great or terrible, in order to maintain a stable level of happiness.

Over time, that means the buzz from a new purchase is pushed toward the emotional norm.

"We stop getting pleasure from it," she says.

And then, of course, we buy new things.

When Ed Diener, a psychology professor at the University of Illinois and a former president of the International Positive Psychology Association — which promotes the study of what lets people lead fulfilling lives — was house-hunting with his wife, they saw several homes with features they liked.

But unlike couples who choose a house because of its open floor plan, fancy kitchens, great light, or spacious bedrooms, Professor Diener arrived at his decision after considering hedonic-adaptation research.

"One home was close to hiking trails, making going hiking very easy," he said in an e-mail. "Thinking about the research, I argued that the hiking trails could be a factor contributing to our happiness, and we should worry less about things like how pretty the kitchen floor is or whether the sinks are fancy. We bought the home near the hiking trail and it has been great, and we haven't tired of this feature because we take a walk four or five days a week."

Scholars have discovered that one way consumers combat hedonic adaptation is to buy many small pleasures instead of one big one. Instead of a new Jaguar, Professor Lyubomirsky advises, buy a massage once a week, have lots of fresh flowers delivered and make phone calls to friends in Europe. Instead of a two-week long vacation, take a few three-day weekends.

"We do adapt to the little things," she says, "but because there's so many, it will take longer."

Before credit cards and cellphones enabled consumers to have almost anything they wanted at any time, the experience of shopping was richer, says Ms. Liebmann of WSL Strategic Retail. "You saved for it, you anticipated it," she says.

In other words, waiting for something and working hard to get it made it feel more valuable and more stimulating.

In fact, scholars have found that anticipation increases happiness. Considering buying an iPad? You might want to think about it as long as possible before taking one home. Likewise about a Caribbean escape: you'll get more pleasure if you book a flight in advance than if you book it at the last minute.

Once upon a time, with roots that go back to medieval market-places featuring stalls that functioned as stores, shopping offered a way to connect socially, as Ms. Liebmann and others have pointed out. But over the last decade, retailing came to be about one thing: unbridled acquisition, epitomized by big-box stores where the mantra was "stack 'em high and let 'em fly" and online transactions that required no social interaction at all — you didn't even have to leave your home.

The recession, however, may force retailers to become reacquainted with shopping's historical roots.

"I think there's a real opportunity in retail to be able to romance the experience again," says Ms. Liebmann. "Retailers are going to have to work very hard to create that emotional feeling again. And it can't just be 'Here's another thing to buy.' It has to have a real sense of experience to it."

Industry professionals say they have difficulty identifying any retailer that is managing to do this well today, with one notable exception: Apple, which offers an interactive retail experience, including classes.

Marie Driscoll, head of the retailing group at Standard & Poor's, says chains have to adapt to new consumer preferences by offering better service, special events and access to designers. Analysts at the Boston Consulting Group advise that companies offer more affordable indulgences, like video games that provide an at-home workout for far less than the cost of a gym membership.

Mr. Cohen of the NPD Group says some companies are doing this. Best Buy is promoting its Geek Squad, promising shoppers before they buy that complicated electronic thingamajig that its employees will hold their hands through the installation process and beyond.

"Nowadays with the economic climate, customers definitely are going for a quality experience," says Nick DeVita, a home entertainment adviser with the Geek Squad. "If they're going to spend their money, they want to make sure it's for the right thing, the right service."

With competition for consumer dollars fiercer than it's been in decades, retailers have had to make the shopping experience more compelling. Mr. Cohen says automakers are offering 30-day test drives, while some clothing stores are promising free personal shoppers. Malls are providing day care while parents shop. Even on the Web, retailers are connecting with customers on Facebook, Twitter and Foursquare, hoping to win their loyalty by offering discounts and invitations to special events.

For the last four years, Roko Belic, a Los Angeles filmmaker, has been traveling the world making a documentary called "Happy." Since beginning work on the film, he has moved to a beach in Malibu from his house in the San Francisco suburbs.

San Francisco was nice, but he couldn't surf there.

"I moved to a trailer park," says Mr. Belic, "which is the first real community that I've lived in in my life." Now he surfs three or four times a week. "It definitely has made me happier," he says. "The things we are trained to think make us happy, like having a new car every couple of years and buying the latest fashions, don't make us happy."

Mr. Belic says his documentary shows that "the one single trait that's common among every single person who is happy is strong relationships."

Buying luxury goods, conversely, tends to be an endless cycle of one-upmanship, in which the neighbors have a fancy new car and — bingo! — now you want one, too, scholars say. A study published in June in Psychological Science by Ms. Dunn and others found that wealth interfered with people's ability to savor positive emotions and experiences, because having an embarrassment of riches reduced the ability to reap enjoyment from life's smaller everyday pleasures, like eating a chocolate bar.

Alternatively, spending money on an event, like camping or a wine tasting with friends, leaves people less likely to compare their experiences with those of others — and, therefore, happier.

Of course, some fashion lovers beg to differ. For many people, clothes will never be more than utilitarian. But for a certain segment of the population, clothes are an art form, a means of self-expression, a way for families to pass down memories through generations. For

Roko Belic surfing in Malibu.

them, studies concluding that people eventually stop deriving pleasure from material things don't ring true.

"No way," says Hayley Corwick, who writes the popular fashion blog Madison Avenue Spy. "I could pull out things from my closet that I bought when I was 17 that I still love."

She rejects the idea that happiness has to be an either-or proposition. Some days, you want a trip, she says; other days, you want a Tom Ford handbag.

Ms. Strobel — our heroine who moved into the 400-square foot apartment — is now an advocate of simple living, writing in her spare time about her own life choices at Rowdykittens.com.

"My lifestyle now would not be possible if I still had a huge two-bedroom apartment filled to the gills with stuff, two cars, and 30 grand in debt," she says.

"Give away some of your stuff," she advises. "See how it feels."

Living With Less. A Lot Less.

OPINION | BY GRAHAM HILL | MARCH 9, 2013

I LIVE IN a 420-square-foot studio. I sleep in a bed that folds down from the wall. I have six dress shirts. I have 10 shallow bowls that I use for salads and main dishes. When people come over for dinner, I pull out my extendable dining room table. I don't have a single CD or DVD and I have 10 percent of the books I once did.

I have come a long way from the life I had in the late '90s, when, flush with cash from an Internet start-up sale, I had a giant house crammed with stuff — electronics and cars and appliances and gadgets.

Somehow this stuff ended up running my life, or a lot of it; the things I consumed ended up consuming me. My circumstances are unusual (not everyone gets an Internet windfall before turning 30), but my relationship with material things isn't.

We live in a world of surfeit stuff, of big-box stores and 24-hour online shopping opportunities. Members of every socioeconomic bracket can and do deluge themselves with products.

There isn't any indication that any of these things makes anyone any happier; in fact it seems the reverse may be true.

For me, it took 15 years, a great love and a lot of travel to get rid of all the inessential things I had collected and live a bigger, better, richer life with less.

It started in 1998 in Seattle, when my partner and I sold our Internet consultancy company, Sitewerks, for more money than I thought I'd earn in a lifetime.

To celebrate, I bought a four-story, 3,600-square-foot, turn-of-the-century house in Seattle's happening Capitol Hill neighborhood and, in a frenzy of consumption, bought a brand-new sectional couch (my first ever), a pair of $300 sunglasses, a ton of gadgets, like an Audible.com MobilePlayer (one of the first portable digital music players) and an audiophile-worthy five-disc CD player. And, of course, a black turbocharged Volvo. With a remote starter!

I was working hard for Sitewerks' new parent company, Bowne, and didn't have the time to finish getting everything I needed for my house. So I hired a guy named Seven, who said he had been Courtney Love's assistant, to be my personal shopper. He went to furniture, appliance and electronics stores and took Polaroids of things he thought I might like to fill the house; I'd shuffle through the pictures and proceed on a virtual shopping spree.

My success and the things it bought quickly changed from novel to normal. Soon I was numb to it all. The new Nokia phone didn't excite me or satisfy me. It didn't take long before I started to wonder why my theoretically upgraded life didn't feel any better and why I felt more anxious than before.

My life was unnecessarily complicated. There were lawns to mow, gutters to clear, floors to vacuum, roommates to manage (it seemed nuts to have such a big, empty house), a car to insure, wash, refuel, repair and register and tech to set up and keep working. To top it all off, I had to keep Seven busy. And really, a personal shopper? Who had I become? My house and my things were my new employers for a job I had never applied for.

It got worse. Soon after we sold our company, I moved east to work in Bowne's office in New York, where I rented a 1,900-square-foot SoHo loft that befit my station as a tech entrepreneur. The new pad needed furniture, housewares, electronics, etc. — which took more time and energy to manage.

And because the place was so big, I felt obliged to get roommates — who required more time, more energy, to manage. I still had the Seattle house, so I found myself worrying about two homes. When I decided to stay in New York, it cost a fortune and took months of cross-country trips — and big headaches — to close on the Seattle house and get rid of the all of the things inside.

I'm lucky, obviously; not everyone gets a windfall from a tech start-up sale. But I'm not the only one whose life is cluttered with excess belongings.

In a study published last year titled "Life at Home in the Twenty-First Century," researchers at U.C.L.A. observed 32 middle-class Los Angeles families and found that all of the mothers' stress hormones spiked during the time they spent dealing with their belongings. Seventy-five percent of the families involved in the study couldn't park their cars in their garages because they were too jammed with things.

Our fondness for stuff affects almost every aspect of our lives. Housing size, for example, has ballooned in the last 60 years. The average size of a new American home in 1950 was 983 square feet; by 2011, the average new home was 2,480 square feet. And those figures don't provide a full picture. In 1950, an average of 3.37 people lived in each American home; in 2011, that number had shrunk to 2.6 people. This means that we take up more than three times the amount of space per capita than we did 60 years ago.

Apparently our supersize homes don't provide space enough for all our possessions, as is evidenced by our country's $22 billion personal storage industry.

What exactly are we storing away in the boxes we cart from place to place? Much of what Americans consume doesn't even find its way into boxes or storage spaces, but winds up in the garbage.

The Natural Resources Defense Council reports, for example, that 40 percent of the food Americans buy finds its way into the trash.

Enormous consumption has global, environmental and social consequences. For at least 335 consecutive months, the average temperature of the globe has exceeded the average for the 20th century. As a recent report for Congress explained, this temperature increase, as well as acidifying oceans, melting glaciers and Arctic Sea ice are "primarily driven by human activity." Many experts believe consumerism and all that it entails — from the extraction of resources to manufacturing to waste disposal — plays a big part in pushing our planet to the brink. And as we saw with Foxconn and the recent Beijing smog scare, many of the affordable products we buy depend on cheap, often exploitive overseas labor and lax environmental regulations.

Does all this endless consumption result in measurably increased happiness?

In a recent study, the Northwestern University psychologist Galen V. Bodenhausen linked consumption with aberrant, antisocial behavior. Professor Bodenhausen found that "Irrespective of personality, in situations that activate a consumer mind-set, people show the same sorts of problematic patterns in well-being, including negative affect and social disengagement." Though American consumer activity has increased substantially since the 1950s, happiness levels have flat-lined.

I don't know that the gadgets I was collecting in my loft were part of an aberrant or antisocial behavior plan during the first months I lived in SoHo. But I was just going along, starting some start-ups that never quite started up when I met Olga, an Andorran beauty, and fell hard. My relationship with stuff quickly came apart.

I followed her to Barcelona when her visa expired and we lived in a tiny flat, totally content and in love before we realized that nothing was holding us in Spain. We packed a few clothes, some toiletries and a couple of laptops and hit the road. We lived in Bangkok, Buenos Aires and Toronto with many stops in between.

A compulsive entrepreneur, I worked all the time and started new companies from an office that fit in my solar backpack. I created some do-gooder companies like We Are Happy to Serve You, which makes a reusable, ceramic version of the iconic New York City Anthora coffee cup and TreeHugger.com, an environmental design blog that I later sold to Discovery Communications. My life was full of love and adventure and work I cared about. I felt free and I didn't miss the car and gadgets and house; instead I felt as if I had quit a dead-end job.

The relationship with Olga eventually ended, but my life never looked the same. I live smaller and travel lighter. I have more time and money. Aside from my travel habit — which I try to keep in check by minimizing trips, combining trips and purchasing carbon offsets — I feel better that my carbon footprint is significantly smaller than in my previous supersized life.

Intuitively, we know that the best stuff in life isn't stuff at all, and that relationships, experiences and meaningful work are the staples of a happy life.

I like material things as much as anyone. I studied product design in school. I'm into gadgets, clothing and all kinds of things. But my experiences show that after a certain point, material objects have a tendency to crowd out the emotional needs they are meant to support.

I wouldn't trade a second spent wandering the streets of Bangkok with Olga for anything I've owned. Often, material objects take up mental as well as physical space.

I'm still a serial entrepreneur, and my latest venture is to design thoughtfully constructed small homes that support our lives, not the other way around. Like the 420-square-foot space I live in, the houses I design contain less stuff and make it easier for owners to live within their means and to limit their environmental footprint. My apartment sleeps four people comfortably; I frequently have dinner parties for 12. My space is well-built, affordable and as functional as living spaces twice the size. As the guy who started TreeHugger.com, I sleep better knowing I'm not using more resources than I need. I have less — and enjoy more.

My space is small. My life is big.

GRAHAM HILL is the founder of LifeEdited.com and TreeHugger.com.

Before You Buy That T-Shirt

OPINION | BY VIKAS BAJAJ | MAY 18, 2013

THE DEATHS AND INJURIES of thousands of garment workers in Bangladesh raise the question of how American and European consumers might assert their power to change appalling factory conditions half a world away. Stop buying clothes made in Bangladesh? Look for labels from other countries, like Indonesia, where conditions might be a little better? Seek out "sweatshop free" clothes, like "fair trade" coffee?

Unfortunately, there are few good answers. A boycott of goods from Bangladesh would probably be counterproductive. It could deprive some of the poorest workers of jobs and income that provide a step up from farming or manual labor. Recent attempts by groups like Fair Trade USA to provide certification for sweatshop-free clothing have gained little traction with retailers or consumers.

Research shows that some American shoppers would prefer and pay more for clothes from factories that don't exploit workers. The problem is that most brands and retailers offer very little information about how their products are made.

Large companies have multilayered supply chains that they change all the time to keep costs low. Production is farmed out to contractors and subcontractors with revolving labor pools. Last year, Walmart claimed that it did not know that a supplier had subcontracted orders to a Bangladeshi factory where more than 112 workers died in a fire.

What can a consumer do when a retailer claims to be in the dark? "Quite honestly the most effective things that consumers can do is really educate themselves about how the things we buy every day are made and ask ourselves do we need 20 T-shirts," said Richard Locke, deputy dean of M.I.T.'s Sloan School of Management.

Mr. Locke argues that our insatiable hunger for cheap clothing in constantly changing styles has created a race to the bottom in which brands perpetually push suppliers in Bangladesh, Cambodia and elsewhere for faster delivery and lower prices. He argues that consumers need to break that cycle by, well, buying less of the cheap, fast fashion in the stores.

That may sound hopelessly idealistic and, at least in the short term, would not necessarily help Bangladeshi workers.

Still, outraged shoppers have successfully pressured companies in the past. In 1992, Nike established a code of conduct for factories that forbade forced labor and child labor — a big problem at the time — and required compliance with local overtime and other labor laws. Mr. Locke's research has found that its efforts have resulted in higher wages and safer working conditions in some factories but not all.

Consumer petitions recently helped persuade several large European companies like H&M to sign a binding agreement with labor groups to improve fire and building safety at Bangladeshi factories. While two American firms, PVH and Abercrombie & Fitch, have also signed on, bigger companies like Walmart and Gap have refused.

The difference in response, said Layna Mosley, a political science professor at the University of North Carolina at Chapel Hill, reflects Europe's greater support in general for unions and labor rights. "U.S. retailers probably think that this is in the news" for now, she said, but that "the dust will settle and it will go back to normal." That's the problem — and it's why consumer power, while an important force, cannot ever fully make up for government failure to enforce labor and safety laws.

VIKAS BAJAJ has worked at The New York Times since 2005. He is a member of the editorial board.

Abundance Without Attachment

OPINION | BY ARTHUR C. BROOKS | DEC. 12, 2014

"CHRISTMAS IS AT our throats again."

That was the cheery yuletide greeting favored by the late English playwright Noël Coward, commemorating the holiday after which he was named. Less contrarian were the words of President Calvin Coolidge: "Christmas is not a time nor a season, but a state of mind. To cherish peace and good will, to be plenteous in mercy, is to have the real spirit of Christmas."

Which quotation strikes a chord with you? Are you a Coward or a Coolidge?

If you sympathize more with Coward, welcome to the club. There are many more of us out there than one might expect. A 2005 survey by the Pew Research Center found that more than half of Americans were bothered "some" or "a lot" by the commercialization of Christmas. A 2013 follow-up confirmed that materialism is Americans' least favorite part of the season.

Call it the Christmas Conundrum. We are supposed to revel in gift-giving and generosity, yet the season's lavishness and commercialization leave many people cold. The underlying contradiction runs throughout modern life. On one hand, we naturally seek and rejoice in prosperity. On the other hand, success in this endeavor is often marred by a materialism we find repellent and alienating.

On a recent trip to India, I found an opportunity to help sort out this contradiction. I sought guidance from a penniless Hindu swami named Gnanmunidas at the Swaminarayan Akshardham Hindu temple in New Delhi. We had never met before, but he came highly recommended by friends. If Yelp reviewed monks, he would have had five stars.

To my astonishment, Gnanmunidas greeted me with an avuncular, "How ya doin'?" He referred to me as "dude." And what was that

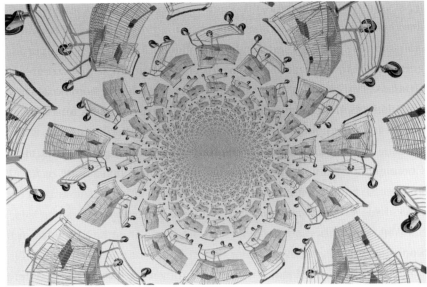

accent — Texas? Sure enough, he had grown up in Houston, the son of Indian petroleum engineers, and had graduated from the University of Texas. Later, he got an M.B.A., and quickly made a lot of money.

But then Gnanmunidas had his awakening. At 26, he asked himself, "Is this all there is?" His grappling with that question led him to India, where he renounced everything and entered a Hindu seminary. Six years later, he emerged a monk. From that moment on, the sum total of his worldly possessions has been two robes, prayer beads and a wooden bowl. He is prohibited from even touching money — a discipline that would obviously be impossible for those of us enmeshed in ordinary economic life.

As an economist, I was more than a little afraid to hear what this capitalist-turned-renunciant had to teach me. But I posed a query nonetheless: "Swami, is economic prosperity a good or bad thing?" I held my breath and waited for his answer.

"It's good," he replied. "It has saved millions of people in my country from starvation."

This was not what I expected. "But you own almost nothing," I pressed. "I was sure you'd say that money is corrupting." He laughed at my naïveté. "There is nothing wrong with money, dude. The problem in life is attachment to money." The formula for a good life, he explained, is simple: abundance without attachment.

The assertion that there is nothing wrong with abundance per se is entirely consistent with most mainstream philosophies. Even traditions commonly perceived as ascetic rarely condemn prosperity on its face. The Dalai Lama, for example, teaches that material goods themselves are not the problem. The real issue, he writes, is our delusion that "satisfaction can arise from gratifying the senses alone."

Moreover, any moral system that takes poverty relief seriously has to celebrate the ahistoric economic bounty that has been harvested these past few centuries. The proportion of the world living on $1 per day or less has shrunk by 80 percent in our lifetimes. Today, Bill Gates can credibly predict that almost no countries will be conventionally "poor" by 2035.

In other words, if we are lucky enough to achieve abundance, we should be thankful for it and work to share the means to create it with others around the world. The real trick is the second part of the formula: avoiding attachment.

In Tibetan, the word "attachment" is translated as "do chag," which literally means "sticky desire." It signifies a desperate grasping at something, motivated by fear of separation from the object. One can find such attachment in many dysfunctional corners of life, from jealous relationships to paranoia about reputation and professional standing.

In the realm of material things, attachment results in envy and avarice. Getting beyond these snares is critical to life satisfaction. But how to do it? Three practices can help.

First, collect experiences, not things.

Material things appear to be permanent, while experiences seem evanescent and likely to be forgotten. Should you take a second honeymoon with your spouse, or get a new couch? The week away sounds great, but hey — the couch is something you'll have forever, right?

Wrong. Thirty years from now, when you are sitting in rocking chairs on the porch, you'll remember your second honeymoon in great detail. But are you likely to say to one another, "Remember that awesome couch?" Of course not. It will be gone and forgotten. Though it seems counterintuitive, it is physically permanent stuff that evaporates from our minds. It is memories in the ether of our consciousness that last a lifetime, there for us to enjoy again and again.

This "paradox of things" has been thoroughly documented by researchers. In 2003, psychologists from the University of Colorado and Cornell studied how Americans remembered different kinds of purchases — material things and experiences — they have made in the past. Using both a national survey and a controlled experiment with human subjects, they found that reflecting on experiential purchases left their subjects significantly happier than did remembering the material acquisitions.

I learned this lesson once and for all from my son Carlos. Five years ago, when Carlos was 9 years old, he announced that all he wanted for Christmas was a fishing trip — just the two of us, alone. No toys; no new things — just the trip. So we went fishing, and have done so every year since. Any material thing I had bought him would have been long forgotten. Yet both of us can tell you every place we've gone together, and all the fish we've caught, every single year.

Second, steer clear of excessive usefulness.

Our daily lives often consist of a dogged pursuit of practicality and usefulness at all costs. This is a sure path toward the attachment we need to avoid. Aristotle makes this point in his Nicomachean Ethics; he shows admiration for learned men because "they knew things that are remarkable, admirable, difficult, and divine, but useless."

Countless studies show that doing things for their own sake — as opposed to things that are merely a means to achieve something else — makes for mindfulness and joy.

In one famous experiment, college students were given puzzles to solve. Some of the students were paid, and others were not. The unpaid participants tended to continue to work on the puzzles after the experiment was finished, whereas the paid participants abandoned the task as soon as the session was over. And the paid subjects reported enjoying the whole experience less.

For those living paycheck to paycheck, a focus on money is understandable. But for those of us blessed to be above poverty, attachment to money is a means-ends confusion. Excessive focus on your finances obscures what you are supposed to enjoy with them. It's as if your experience of the holidays never extended beyond the time spent at the airport on the way to see family. (If you're thinking that's actually the best part, then you have a different problem.)

This manifestly does not mean we should abandon productive impulses. On the contrary, it means we need to treat our industry as an intrinsic end. This is the point made famously in the Hindu text the Bhagavad Gita, where work is sanctified as inherently valuable, not as a path to a payoff.

And finally, get to the center of the wheel.

In the rose windows of many medieval churches, one finds the famous "wheel of fortune," or rota fortunae. The concept is borrowed from ancient Romans' worship of the pagan goddess Fortuna. Following the wheel's rim around, one sees the cycle of victory and defeat that everyone experiences throughout the struggles of life. At the top of the circle is a king; at the bottom, the same man as a pauper.

Chaucer's "Canterbury Tales" uses the idea to tell of important people brought low throughout history: "And thus does Fortune's wheel turn treacherously. And out of happiness bring men to sorrow."

The lesson went beyond the rich and famous. Everyone was supposed to remember that each of us is turning on the wheel. One day, we're at the top of our game. But from time to time, we find ourselves laid low in health, wealth and reputation.

If the lesson ended there, it would be pretty depressing. Every victory seems an exercise in futility, because soon enough we will be back at the bottom. But as the Catholic theologian Robert Barron writes, the early church answered this existential puzzle by placing Jesus at the center of the wheel. Worldly things occupy the wheel's rim. These objects of attachment spin ceaselessly and mercilessly. Fixed at the center was the focal point of faith, the lodestar for transcending health, wealth, power, pleasure and fame — for moving beyond mortal abundance. The least practical thing in life was thus the most important and enduring.

But even if you are not religious, there is an important lesson for us embedded in this ancient theology. Namely, woe be unto those who live and die by the slings and arrows of worldly attachment. To prioritize these things is to cling to the rim, a sure recipe for existential vertigo. Instead, make sure you know what is the transcendental truth at the center of your wheel, and make that your focus.

So here is my central claim: The frustration and emptiness so many people feel at this time of year is not an objection to the abundance per se, nor should it be. It is a healthy hunger for nonattachment. This season, don't rail against the crowds of shoppers on Fifth Avenue or become some sort of anti-gift misanthrope. Celebrate the bounty that has pulled millions out of poverty worldwide. But then, ponder the three practices above. Move beyond attachment by collecting experiences, avoid excessive usefulness, and get to the center of your wheel. It might just turn out to be a happy holiday after all.

I never finished my story about Swami Gnanmunidas. Before I left him that day in Delhi, we had a light lunch of soup and naan. I told him I would be writing about our conversation; many Americans would be hearing his name. He contemplated this for a moment and, modeling nonattachment, responded simply.

"Dude, do you like the soup? It's spicy."

ARTHUR C. BROOKS is a contributing opinion writer who is the president of the American Enterprise Institute.

Small Shops Take Pride in Turning Their Backs on Black Friday

BY STACY COWLEY | NOV. 25, 2015

ON BLACK FRIDAY, as hordes of people begin their holiday shopping rites, Nan Morningstar will keep the door closed at Free Radicals, the clothing and costume boutique she and her husband own in Albuquerque.

To make absolutely sure that no one can buy anything from her that day, she also plans to disable the shopping cart on her store's website.

"It seems like it's been getting more overblown in America, and more out of hand," she said of the annual post-Thanksgiving sales rush. "We don't want to participate."

As big-box retailers prepare for their "doorbuster" sales and ever earlier opening hours, some small businesses are making a point of going to the other extreme. They are shunning discounts and avoiding extended hours, especially those that cut into the Thanksgiving holiday.

Some, like Ms. Morningstar, are explicit about their desire to fight the holiday season's commercialization. Lesouque, an online seller of globally sourced accessories and home goods, is closing its website for the day as part of a "break up with Black Friday" campaign, and it won't be offering any discounts during the holiday season.

Gokben Yamandag, a co-founder of the site, spent years as a textile engineer at factories in Turkey, watching teenagers work long hours in harsh conditions. She came away from the experience with a deep horror of the marketing frenzies that encourage people to buy products in bulk at deep discounts.

"These lower prices come with hidden costs," she said. "Consumers might not know that when they buy their 'two for $10' shirts, someone along the way is paying the price. In most cases, the one paying is the person making our clothes."

Other retailers simply see closing for Black Friday as a sensible business choice.

At Curds and Wine, a San Diego shop that sells winemaking and cheesemaking supplies, Rebecca Mershon demonstrates a step in making wine. The store shuts for the week around Thanksgiving.

"People just don't go to small businesses. They go to big-box stores looking for big, super deals," said Gisela Claassen, the owner of Curds and Wine, a San Diego shop that sells winemaking and cheesemaking supplies. "The first year I was open, I had nothing to do. Nobody came in."

Ms. Claassen now shuts her store for the entire week around Thanksgiving. "My employees love it," she said. "They get to spend the time with their families."

There is some evidence to back Ms. Claassen's belief that most holiday shoppers are not drawn to businesses like hers. Only 24 percent of those planning to make holiday purchases say they intend to buy them from small local retailers, according to a National Retail Federation report. The organization forecasts that holiday sales will rise 3.7 percent this year, to $630.5 billion.

Some independent stores opening for the season's earliest shopping hours are doing it grudgingly. As major retailers like Macy's,

Sears and Target have moved their hours ever earlier — this year, all three will open at 6 p.m. on Thanksgiving Day — a growing number of malls are following their anchor tenants' leads and opening on the evening of the holiday after being closed all day. Some require all of their merchants to adhere to the schedule.

Deer Creek Winery, a family-run winemaker in Shippenville, Pa., has outlets in four Pennsylvania malls. Rhonda Brooks, a co-owner of the winery, would prefer to keep all of the stores closed on Thanksgiving, but two of the malls, Clearview Mall in Butler and Shenango Valley Mall in Hermitage, issued mandates telling tenants to open at 6 p.m. or risk being fined.

Deer Creek heeded Clearview's rule two years ago and opened on Thursday night. Sales were slow — "people only wanted to be at the big-box stores, for all the big sales," Ms. Brooks said — and employees complained about having to leave their families to go to work.

Last year, she refused, putting up a sign a week in advance saying that the store would not be open. Clearview did not levy a fine, Ms. Brooks said. (A representative of Clearview did not respond to a request for comment.)

But at Shenango Valley, where Deer Creek's store opened a few months ago, she felt compelled to follow her new landlord's rules. Her store will open at 6 p.m.

Paul Vidwan, the mall's general manager, said most retailers were in favor of the policy.

"If we are pushing this and promoting this and advertising that we're open, it's not very good for us if half the stores are closed," he said.

The fines for those who flout the rule vary at Shenango Valley Mall, depending on the details of each tenant's lease. Dale Willerton, a former mall manager who now runs a commercial lease consulting business, said mall fines for offenses like ignoring holiday hours typically ran around $200 a day. He noted that most managers did not follow through with their threats to charge the fines.

Black Friday has become synonymous with heavy discounting, but small businesses can rarely afford to slash prices the way the big chains do — and some refuse to even try. Courtney Stamm, the owner of the Cheeky Puppy, a pet goods boutique in Washington, plans to open on Black Friday, but she will not be running any sales or promotions.

"Our customers are not particularly motivated by discounts," she said. "There are times that I've put items on a sale shelf and they just sit there."

She is instead focusing her energy on the day after Black Friday, which a campaign led by American Express promotes as Small Business Saturday. In past years, American Express has given its customers statement credits of $10 to $25 for making purchases that day at participating small retailers. The company said it would not offer any refunds this year, but it is continuing to publicize the event.

To draw in Saturday shoppers, Ms. Stamm arranges special events. Last year, she brought in a popular Etsy seller of custom collars and leashes to take on-site orders; the day set a sales record for her business. This year, a professional pet photographer will be at the store to snap portraits in return for a $20 donation to a local rescue group.

Some online retailers are also holding out against the seasonal pressure for discounts.

Tuft & Needle, an online mattress retailer, advertises on Facebook, where the ads' viewers are free to leave comments. For weeks, one question has come up there repeatedly: What holiday sales are you offering?

The answer is none. The company experimented in the past with small referral discounts and found that the customers they brought in had higher return rates and lower satisfaction scores. The company's founders, who preferred to set one price and stick to it, decided their mattresses would never go on sale.

"It's crazy how trained the shoppers are now," said Evan Maridou, Tuft & Needle's chief operating officer. Even without discounts, last year's Monday after Thanksgiving was its biggest sales day of the year.

In Albuquerque, Ms. Morningstar plans to avoid shopping at all on Black Friday. Instead, she will eat leftovers and spend time with her family and friends.

"This is one of the perks of being a microbusiness," she said. "Since I'm the boss, I get to say if we're going to take a day off."

Let Consumers Sue Companies

OPINION | BY RICHARD CORDRAY | AUG. 22, 2017

WASHINGTON — When a data breach at Home Depot in 2014 led to losses for banks nationwide, a group of banks filed a class-action lawsuit seeking compensation. Companies have the choice of taking legal action together. Yet consumers are frequently blocked from exercising the same legal right when they believe that companies have wronged them.

That's because many contracts for products like credit cards and bank accounts have mandatory arbitration clauses that prevent consumers from joining group lawsuits, forcing them to go it alone. For example, a group lawsuit against Wells Fargo for secretly opening phony bank accounts was blocked by arbitration clauses that pushed individual consumers into closed-door proceedings.

In 2010, the Consumer Financial Protection Bureau, which I direct, was authorized to study mandatory arbitration and write rules consistent with the study. After five years of work, we recently finalized a rule to stop companies from denying groups of consumers the option of going to court when they are treated unfairly.

Opponents have unleashed attacks to overturn the rule, and the House just passed legislation to that end. Before the Senate decides whether to protect companies or consumers, it's worth correcting the record.

First, opponents claim that plaintiffs are better served by acting individually than by joining a group lawsuit. This claim is not supported by facts or common sense. Our study contained revealing data on the results of group lawsuits and individual actions. We found that group lawsuits get more money back to more people. In five years of group lawsuits, we tallied an average of $220 million paid to 6.8 million consumers per year. Yet in the arbitration cases we studied, on average, 16 people per year recovered less than $100,000 total.

Wells Fargo ATM machines.

It is true that the average payouts are higher in individual suits. But that is because very few people go through arbitration, and they generally do so only when thousands of dollars are at stake, whereas the typical group lawsuit seeks to recover small amounts for many people. Almost nobody spends time or money fighting a small fee on their own. As one judge noted, "only a lunatic or a fanatic sues for $30."

When a bank charges illegal fees to millions of customers and then blocks them from suing together, a result is not millions of individual claims, but zero. So the bank gets to pocket millions in ill-gotten gains.

Not only do group lawsuits help consumers recover money they otherwise would forfeit, but they also protect many more consumers by halting and deterring harmful behavior. For example, when banks reordered bank debits to charge more overdraft fees, consumers sued and recovered $1 billion. Most banks have since stopped the practice.

Our rule does not ban individual arbitration, as our opponents falsely claim. It simply ensures that consumers have the option of joining together to sue companies. Companies and consumers can still use arbitration to resolve their differences, but companies cannot unilaterally block group lawsuits.

Opponents also claim that the rule benefits lawyers rather than consumers. In reality, lawyers collect a small portion compared with consumers, and only if they succeed. For every $10 that a company pays out for wrongdoing, we found about $8 goes to consumers and $2 goes to pay legal costs. In any event, banks choose to hire lawyers to file class-action lawsuits, and ordinary people deserve to make the same choice.

Finally, this rule does not risk the safety or soundness of the banking system. We estimate the potential costs of this rule for the entire financial system at under $1 billion per year, whereas banks alone made $171 billion in profits last year. The law already bans mandatory arbitration clauses in financial contracts for military service members and in mortgages (the largest consumer financial market), yet the financial sector remains strong.

In truth, by blocking group lawsuits, mandatory arbitration clauses eliminate a powerful means to get justice when a little harm happens to a lot of people. It is the height of hypocrisy for companies to say they're helping consumers by closing off the very same legal option they use when they've been wronged.

A cherished tenet of our justice system is that nobody should escape accountability for breaking the law. Our rule restores consumers' legal right to stand up for themselves and have their day in court without having to wait on the government to act. That is an idea everyone should support.

RICHARD CORDRAY is the director of the Consumer Financial Protection Bureau.

My Year of No Shopping

OPINION | BY ANN PATCHETT | DEC. 15, 2017

NASHVILLE — The idea began in February 2009 over lunch with my friend Elissa, someone I like but rarely see. She walked into the restaurant wearing a fitted black coat with a high collar.

"Wow," I said admiringly. "Some coat."

She stroked the sleeve. "Yeah. I bought it at the end of my no-shopping year. I still feel a little bad about it."

Elissa told me the story: After traveling for much of the previous year, she had decided she had enough stuff, or too much stuff. She made a pledge that for 12 months she wouldn't buy shoes, clothes, purses or jewelry.

I was impressed by her discipline, but she shrugged it off. "It wasn't hard."

I did some small-scale experiments of my own, giving up shopping for Lent for a few years. I was always surprised by how much better it made me feel. But it wasn't until last New Year's Day that I decided to follow my friend's example.

At the end of 2016, our country had swung in the direction of gold leaf, an ecstatic celebration of unfeeling billionaire-dom that kept me up at night. I couldn't settle down to read or write, and in my anxiety I found myself mindlessly scrolling through two particular shopping websites, numbing my fears with pictures of shoes, clothes, purses and jewelry. I was trying to distract myself, but the distraction left me feeling worse, the way a late night in a bar smoking Winstons and drinking gin leaves you feeling worse. The unspoken question of shopping is "What do I need?" What I needed was less.

My plan had been to give up what Elissa gave up — things to wear — but a week into my no-shopping year, I bought a portable speaker. When I got it home I felt ridiculous. Shouldn't "no shopping" include electronics?

I came up with my own arbitrary set of rules for the year. I wanted a plan that was serious but not so draconian that I would bail out in February, so while I couldn't buy clothing or speakers, I could buy anything in the grocery store, including flowers. I could buy shampoo and printer cartridges and batteries but only after I'd run out of what I had. I could buy plane tickets and eat out in restaurants. I could buy books because I write books and I co-own a bookstore and books are my business. Could I have made it a full year without buying books? Absolutely. I could have used the library or read the books that were already in my house, but I didn't; I bought books.

Gifts were the tough one for me. I'm a gift-giver, and I could see how gift shopping could become an easy loophole. I decided to give books as gifts, but I didn't always keep to it. My editor married in 2017, and I wasn't about to give him a book as a wedding present. Still, the frantic shopping for others needed to come to a halt. The idea that our affection and esteem must manifest itself in yet another sweater is reductive. Elissa said she gave people time, a certificate to watch their kids or clean their house. "That," she told me, "turned out to be the hardest thing. Time is so valuable."

I was raised Catholic and spent 12 years in a Catholic girls school. In the same way a child who grows up going to the symphony is more likely to enjoy classical music, and a child raised in a bilingual household is probably going to speak two languages, many children raised Catholic have a talent for self-denial. Even now my sister and I plan for Lent the way other people plan family vacations: What will we let go of? What good can we add?

My first few months of no shopping were full of gleeful discoveries. I ran out of lip balm early on and before making a decision about whether lip balm constituted a need, I looked in my desk drawers and coat pockets. I found five lip balms. Once I started digging around under the bathroom sink I realized I could probably run this experiment for three more years before using up all the lotion, soap and dental floss. It turns out I hadn't thrown away the hair products and face creams I'd bought over the years and didn't like; I'd just tossed them all under the sink.

I'm using them now, and they're fine.

In March I wished I had a Fitbit, the new one that looked like a bracelet and didn't need to be connected to a smartphone. For four days I really wanted a Fitbit. And then — *poof!* — I didn't want one. I remember my parents trying to teach me this lesson when I was a child: If you want something, wait awhile. Chances are the feeling will pass.

The trick of no shopping isn't just that you don't buy things. You don't *shop*. That means no trawling the sale section of the J. Crew website in idle moments. It means the catalogs go into the recycle bin unopened on the theory that if I don't see it, I don't want it. Halfway through the year I could go to a store with my mother and sister if they asked me. I could tell them if the dress they were trying on looked good without wishing I could try it on myself.

Not shopping saves an astonishing amount of time. In October, I interviewed Tom Hanks about his collection of short stories in front of 1,700 people in a Washington theater. Previously, I would have believed that such an occasion demanded a new dress and lost two days of my life looking for one. In fact, Tom Hanks had never seen any of my dresses, nor had the people in the audience. I went to my closet, picked out something weather appropriate and stuck it in my suitcase. Done.

I did a favor for a friend over the summer and she bought me a pair of tennis shoes. Her simple act of kindness thrilled me. Once I stopped looking for things to buy, I became tremendously grateful for the things I received. Had I been shopping this summer I would have told my friend, "You shouldn't have," and I would have meant it.

It doesn't take so long for a craving to subside, be it for Winstons or gin or cupcakes. Once I got the hang of giving shopping up, it wasn't much of a trick. The trickier part was living with the startling abundance that had become glaringly obvious when I stopped trying to get more. Once I could see what I already had, and what actually mattered, I was left with a feeling that was somewhere between sickened and humbled. When did I amass so many things, and did someone else need them?

If you stop thinking about what you might want, it's a whole lot easier to see what other people don't have. There's a reason that just about every religion regards material belongings as an impediment to peace. This is why Siddhartha had to leave his palace to become the Buddha. This is why Jesus said, "Blessed are the poor." It's why my friend Sister Nena, an 85-year-old Catholic nun, took a vow of poverty when she entered the convent at 18.

Sister Nena was my reading teacher when I was in the first grade, and in the years since, she has taught me considerably more. When I ask her if there's anything she needs me to get for her, she shakes her head. "It's all just stuff," she says, meaning all of the things that aren't God. If you're in the market for genuine inspiration on this front, I urge you to read "Barking to the Choir: The Power of Radical Kinship," by Gregory Boyle, a book that shows what the platitudes of faith look like when they're put into action.

The things we buy and buy and buy are like a thick coat of Vaseline smeared on glass: We can see some shapes out there, light and dark, but in our constant craving for what we may still want, we miss life's details. It's not as if I kept a ledger and took the money I didn't spend on perfume and gave that money to the poor, but I came to a better understanding of money as something we earn and spend and save for the things we want and need. Once I was able to get past the want and be honest about the need, it was easier to give more of my money to people who could really use it.

For the record, I still have more than plenty. I know there is a vast difference between not buying things and not being able to buy things. Not shopping for a year hardly makes me one with the poor, but it has put me on the path of figuring out what I can do to help. I understand that buying things is the backbone of the economy and job growth. I appreciate all the people who shop in the bookstore. But taking some time off from consumerism isn't going to make the financial markets collapse. If you're looking for a New Year's resolution, I have to tell you: This one's great.

What I still haven't figured out is how the experiment ends. Do I just start shopping again? Shop less? I called Elissa. I hadn't seen her in years. She told me that after she bought the black coat, she decided to re-up for another year.

"I realized I had too many decisions to make that were actually important," she said. "There were people to help, things to do. Not shopping frees up a lot of space in your brain."

So for now I'll leave my pledge in place. Who knows how far I can go? In a country hellbent on selling us dresses and shirts with the shoulders cut out (though I like to think I wouldn't have fallen for that one even if I had been shopping), it's good to sit on the bench for a while. Or as the great social activist Dorothy Day liked to say, "The best thing to do with the best things in life is give them up."

ANN PATCHETT is the author, most recently, of the novel "Commonwealth" and the co-owner of Parnassus Books.

How Consumers Can Resist Companies' Market Power

COLUMN | BY AUSTAN GOOLSBEE | JULY 20, 2018

The Economic View column explores life through an economic lens with leading economists and writers.

A BASIC RULE of economics is that the price depends on how willing consumers are to buy something else.

The less consumers pay attention when they buy — and the more they just follow a set shopping pattern — the greater the market power possessed by the seller, and the more that seller can charge.

Modern companies know this very well, and they do what they can to improve their advantages over unwary consumers.

I've unwittingly been caught in consumer traps myself.

About 15 years ago, for example, my wife and I decided to send out holiday cards using an online photo service rather than writing them out and sending them by hand. We picked Shutterfly, which did a good job. And we're still using it, largely because after we had typed 100 addresses into the Shutterfly site, it would have taken a heck of a deal to persuaded us to type them in again somewhere else.

So the truth is we haven't bothered to shop around much. We've just stuck with Shutterfly, and that is undoubtedly costing us money.

Economists have thought a lot about markets like the one exemplified by Shutterfly — those with significant "switching costs" and "lock-in effects."

In such markets, companies should be extremely generous up front trying to earn your business, knowing you will be stuck with them. And, in theory, you will think about their future market power carefully when you first decide whether to sign up. That's what a rational, forward-looking consumer should do.

But that theory might not describe the actual marketplace that well. When my wife and I chose Shutterfly, we didn't really think about what competitors might exist 14 years later or how the prices might change once they got us signed up in 2004.

We probably should have thought about all of that, realizing that, down the road, cloud storage prices would become immensely cheaper and we could get better deals if we maintained our flexibility. Instead, we bumbled our way into giving a company the power to monopolize us.

That kind of thing happens a lot these days. People make quick shopping decisions that have long-term consequences.

Let's say you bought an Alexa to help with tasks around the house. Did you know that Alexa would also consistently try to steer your purchases to Amazon's house brands when you asked her to order something? Maybe not, but you gave Alexa market power the moment you plugged her in.

Big companies know that the more convenient they make their product or service, the less you will shop around and the more market power they will have. Plus they've gotten good at tailoring products to certain consumers to get them to give up comparison shopping altogether.

In a fascinating new analysis, the economists Brent Neiman and Joseph Vavra at the University of Chicago Booth School of Business studied data on 700 million purchases in grocery and big-box stores for 160,000 households over more than a decade to determine how specialized American consumers have become when they make purchases.

The researchers (who are, incidentally, my friends and colleagues) found that while companies sell many more products than before, as individuals we are increasingly buying only our one favored product in a given category. In other words, we are not comparison shopping or forcing companies to compete for business.

Take the case of tortilla chips. Fifteen years ago, Tostitos dominated all other chip makers, but sometimes consumers would buy Mission chips or a local brand if they were cheaper or the mood struck them.

Today, Tostitos is still the dominant brand but has expanded into 13 specialized varieties like Tostitos Hint of Lime, Tostitos Bite Size and Tostitos Multigrain. It also has five party sizes, four Simply Tostitos organic or sea-salted varieties and three different Tostitos Cantina styles.

Today, the same consumer tends to go into the store looking just to buy one of the specialized varieties of Tostitos: She really loves Hint of Lime or is intent on buying Tostitos Scoops (chips in the shape of tiny taco bowls). People don't try alternatives the way they used to. They act as if they are locked in.

On the one hand, consumers shouldn't complain about this. After all, Tostitos (or Frito-Lay, the Pepsi subsidiary that owns Tostitos) created lots of new products that people like better. That's innovation. Good for them.

But this innovation comes with a downside. The more specific consumer tastes get, the more the companies can exploit their ability to cater to those tastes without competition. The Neiman and Vavra study shows exactly what you would expect: The more specialized the demand, the higher the prices people pay and the greater the market power possessed by a company.

Creating specialized demand is an intriguing way of locking customers into a product. Another method is selling a discount subscription — cable, magazines, pest control — that automatically renews at a higher price. Consumers have to remember and make the effort to cancel if they want to shop around. Companies offer convenience, but they make the consumers pay for it.

These behavioral traps may seem far removed from the macro-level discussions of market power that dominate economic analysis such as the staggering increases in corporate earnings and profit margins and the simultaneous stagnation of wages. Economists often argue whether the underlying causes of these phenomena are lax anti-trust enforcement, rapid technological development, globalization, declining unions or other factors.

But even as we debate these larger notions, let us not forget the ways in which we, consumers at the very base of the economy, increase corporate market power with the ways we shop.

That isn't meant to deny the importance of conventional macroeconomic factors in the rise of market power. And it certainly isn't meant to play down the role that could be played by government policy like more aggressive antitrust enforcement, consumer protection or regulation.

But beyond the effects of government or technology or globalization, individual choices matter. Companies don't want you to comparison shop, which could force them to compete for your business. They want you to develop regular shopping habits. The more people do that, the higher the prices everyone will pay.

I try to remember that when I shop now. I remind myself not to just buy the first thing listed on a website or displayed on the rack at the checkout aisle. When I take a ride-hailing service, I will check both Uber and Lyft before choosing. Sometimes I check the price of things online without logging in or shift my browser to private mode to see if a company is offering better deals to new customers.

For an individual shopper, these actions are a bit of a pain, and they may not do much to improve matters over all. But if enough people behave this way — keeping companies guessing and making them work for our business — these small acts of consumer resistance can help keep corporate market power in check.

AUSTAN GOOLSBEE, a professor of economics at the University of Chicago's Booth School of Business, was an adviser to President Barack Obama.

'Friday Black' Uses Fantasy and Blistering Satire to Skewer Racism and Consumer Culture

REVIEW | BY ALEXANDRA ALTER | OCT. 19, 2018

Nana Kwame Adjei-Brenyah's debut story collection has been compared to works by literary masters like Isaac Babel, Ralph Ellison and Anton Chekhov.

IN "FRIDAY BLACK," the title story in Nana Kwame Adjei-Brenyah's strange, dark and sometimes unnervingly funny debut collection, a shopping mall turns into a site of carnage as rabid shoppers stampede through the aisles of a clothing store in pursuit of discounted winter wear. The narrator, an unflappable salesman, calmly tosses fleece jackets into the frenzied crowd as trampled, mangled bodies accumulate.

The story is a not-so-subtle critique of consumerism run amok. But like all effective satire, there's a glint of truth and accumulation of mundane details that make the farcical scenario feel plausible.

Like his narrator, Mr. Adjei-Brenyah had to contend with ravenous shoppers during the holiday season, back when he worked in a clothing store at the Palisades mall in West Nyack, N.Y.

"I've seen somebody step on someone else to get the jeans on a Black Friday," he said, still sounding confounded by the behavior he witnessed. "How did you decide to step on a human being to get a pair of jeans?"

Similarly simple but profound questions animate the other stories in "Friday Black," which uses fantasy and scorching satire to tackle issues like school shootings, abortion, racism, the callowness of commercialism, and how cyclical violence can be passed on across generations.

Most of the stories take place in prosaic settings — shopping malls, theme parks, hospitals, suburban neighborhoods, college campus

"Sometimes hyperbole comes from saying the truth plainly," Mr. Adjei-Brenyah said. "It helps me get directly to the point."

libraries — but Mr. Adjei-Brenyah renders prosaic scenarios unfamiliar by adding a surreal, disorienting twist.

"Sometimes hyperbole comes from saying the truth plainly," Mr. Adjei-Brenyah said. "It helps me get directly to the point."

In "The Finkelstein 5," the first story in the collection, Mr. Adjei-Brenyah takes this approach to its extreme conclusion. To write about the experience of code-switching as a young black man, he gives the protagonist, Emmanuel, the ability to dial his "Blackness" up or down in different situations. He adjusts his Blackness to 1.5 for a phone call with a prospective employer, and raises it to a 10 when he joins a radical protest movement. He's come to expect routine racism — like a security guard demanding to see a receipt after he buys clothing in a store. But he's moved to action by a grotesque act of brutality, after a man who decapitated five black children with a chain-saw gets acquitted by a jury.

By making the murders so vicious and extreme, Mr. Adjei-Brenyah manages both to deliver a shock, and to point out our diminished capacity to experience shock at the routine violence against unarmed African-Americans.

"If I see someone who looks like me getting murdered with impunity, that feels like something I should talk about," he said. "Just how bad does it have to be for us to care?"

During a recent interview, a few weeks ahead of the book's release, Mr. Adjei-Brenyah, 27, gushed about his favorite writers — "Toni Morrison is God," he said, seemingly without intending hyperbole — and was stunned by the growing tsunami of praise "Friday Black" has generated. The collection has been compared to works by literary titans like Isaac Babel, Ralph Ellison, Anton Chekhov and Kurt Vonnegut, and has drawn ecstatic blurbs from Mary Karr, Dana Spiotta, Charles Yu and Roxane Gay, who called it "dark and captivating and essential."

Mr. Adjei-Brenyah grew up in Spring Valley, N.Y., the son of Ghanaian immigrants. As a boy, he devoured science fiction and fantasy and Japanese Manga. Later, as an undergraduate at the

University at Albany, SUNY, he made his first attempt at writing for a wider audience. After learning of yet another police shooting of a young African-American, he stayed up all night writing a pamphlet denouncing systemic racism, which he printed and scattered around the campus.

"I went to bed at 5 a.m. that morning thinking, well, I fixed racism," he said. "I basically just littered all over the campus."

The pamphlet got little attention. But Mr. Adjei-Brenyah became determined to find a vehicle for his ideas, a medium that would both entertain readers and deliver a blunt message. "Part of me was like, how do you make people read it?" he said.

He took a writing workshop with the novelist Lynne Tillman, who urged him to read works by George Saunders, James Baldwin and Grace Paley, among others.

"In this very ferocious period we're living in, in a period of great binaries, he's able to find another way to talk about these issues we're facing," Ms. Tillman said.

Some of his early stories were about working in retail, something he knew a fair bit about from the years he spent working at a clothing store in the Palisades mall and later at the Crossgates Mall outside Albany. In some ways, being a salesman was good preparation for being a writer. He became a keen observer of people's moods and mannerisms. He learned how to intuit both what they wanted and what they could afford, and how to read into the details of how people dressed and where their eyes lingered.

"I can upsell, I can downsell," he said. "A lot of it is noticing what people are noticing."

One Black Friday weekend, he sold about $17,000 worth of North Face jackets, he said. As a reward, he got a free North Face jacket for his mother, a detail he slipped into the story "How to Sell a Jacket as Told by IceKing," which is narrated by an adept salesman who gets a free PoleFace jacket for his mom after selling almost $18,000 worth of merchandise.

There were grim moments at the mall that shaped his fiction too. About a decade ago, when Mr. Adjei-Brenyah was working at the mall, someone fell from one of the mall's upper floors and died, in a likely suicide — an event that he alludes to in his short story, "In Retail." The hum of shoppers shopping halted briefly, but resumed after the body was taken away.

When he got to the graduate writing program at Syracuse University, where he now teaches, Mr. Adjei-Brenyah first tried writing realistic stories — "because I wanted to be taken seriously" — but fantasy started seeping into his work. He read Ishmael Reed's experimental satire "Mumbo Jumbo," and something clicked. "I didn't realize you could be so irreverent in talking about these issues," he said. He saw he could use magical realism, or something like it, to write about the issues that had always preoccupied him — race and the depravities of consumer culture and our collective habituation to violence.

He enrolled in a writing workshop with Mr. Saunders, a contemporary master of fiction that teeters on the edge of otherworldliness, who became a mentor to him. One of the first stories he submitted to Mr. Saunders was a draft of "The Finkelstein 5."

"It was just a mindblower," Mr. Saunders said. "As fantastical as the story is, it's referring to reality. Racism is real, and that's what it feels like from the inside."

Another story he showed Mr. Saunders, "Zimmer Land," unfolds in a theme park where patrons pay to act out their racist revenge fantasies on actors impersonating "thugs" and terrorists. Before he finished it, Mr. Adjei-Brenyah asked Mr. Saunders if he minded him using a theme park setting, since Mr. Saunders is famous for, among other things, writing fiction set in creepy theme parks. Mr. Saunders gave his hearty approval.

"This is a person who's using fiction to ask and answer big, urgent questions," Mr. Saunders said. "That's why the stories feel new, because they're compressed tools for moral exploration."

The 12 stories in "Friday Black" veer between pure realism and straight-up science fiction, and something in between. The juxtaposition feels casual rather than deliberate, perhaps because Mr. Adjei-Brenyah finds distinctions between literary and genre fiction, and between fantasy and reality, meaningless.

In one of the more personal stories in the collection, "The Hospital Where," the narrator is tending to his sick father when he is confronted by a god with 12 tongues, a demonic muse of sorts who compels him to write stories.

That's what it feels like to him when the urge to write strikes, like an almost supernatural possession, Mr. Adjei-Brenyah said.

In the story, the deity issues a command to the aspiring writer before she leaves.

"Don't be boring," the god admonishes him.

Glossary

analog Relating to a physical quantity; the opposite of digital.

antitrust Legislation intended to promote competition in business by preventing trusts or monopolies.

barrage To bombard someone with something.

big-box A large store that sells wares at discount prices, usually as part of a chain of stores such as Walmart, Target, etc.

capitalism An economic and political system that has trade and industry controlled by private owners and corporations and operated for profit, rather than by the state.

carbon footprint The amount of carbon dioxide emitted due to the use of fossil fuels by a particular person or group.

commercialism Practices that emphasize the maximizing of profit, occasionally at the expense of quality.

connoisseur A person who is an expert and able to pass judgment in matters of taste.

consumerism A belief that the expansion of goods consumption is good for the economy; the protection of consumer interests.

deficit The amount by which a sum of money is too small.

demographics Statistical data of human populations, such as age or income.

discretionary spending Money spent by consumers on non-essential items such as vacations or luxury items.

draconian Excessively harsh or severe, particular in terms of laws and their application.

ephemeral Lasting for a short period of time.

frugality Being economical or thrifty with food or money.

hierarchy A system in which things are organized according to importance or rank.

homogeneity The quality or state of being the same or of a similar kind.

luddite A person opposed to technology or new ways of working.

macroeconomics The part of economics concerned with large-scale factors such as interest rates and productivity.

materialism The tendency to consider material possessions and physical comfort as having more importance than spiritual values.

millennial The generation or demographic cohort containing individuals born between the early 1980s and late 1990s.

recession A period of temporary economic decline measured by a country's gross domestic product.

supply and demand A fundamental concept of economics that speaks to the relationship between the amount of a product available and the desire of buyers.

utilitarian Something that is designed to be useful or practical rather than attractive.

Media Literacy Terms

"Media literacy" refers to the ability to access, understand, critically assess and create media. The following terms are important components of media literacy, and they will help you critically engage with the articles in this title.

angle The aspect of a news story that a journalist focuses on and develops.

attribution The method by which a source is identified or by which facts and information are assigned to the person who provided them.

balance Principle of journalism that both perspectives of an argument should be presented in a fair way.

bias A disposition of prejudice in favor of a certain idea, person or perspective.

column A type of story that is a regular feature, often on a recurring topic, written by the same journalist, generally known as a columnist.

commentary A type of story that is an expression of opinion on recent events by a journalist generally known as a commentator.

credibility The quality of being trustworthy and believable, said of a journalistic source.

critical review A type of story that describes an event or work of art, such as a theater performance, film, concert, book, restaurant, radio or television program, exhibition or musical piece, and offers critical assessment of its quality and reception.

editorial Article of opinion or interpretation.

fake news A fictional or made-up story presented in the style of a legitimate news story, intended to deceive readers; also commonly used to criticize legitimate news because of its perspective or unfavorable coverage of a subject.

feature story Article designed to entertain as well as to inform.

impartiality Principle of journalism that a story should not reflect a journalist's bias and should contain balance.

intention The motive or reason behind something, such as the publication of a news story.

motive The reason behind something, such as the publication of a news story or a source's perspective on an issue.

op-ed An opinion piece that reflects a prominent individual's opinion on a topic of interest.

paraphrase The summary of an individual's words, with attribution, rather than a direct quotation of their exact words.

plagiarism An attempt to pass another person's work as one's own without attribution.

quotation The use of an individual's exact words indicated by the use of quotation marks and proper attribution.

reliability The quality of being dependable and accurate, said of a journalistic source.

rhetorical device Technique in writing intending to persuade the reader or communicate a message from a certain perspective.

style A distinctive use of language in writing or speech; also a news or publishing organization's rules for consistent use of language with regard to spelling, punctuation, typography and capitalization, usually regimented by a house style guide.

tone A manner of expression in writing or speech.

Media Literacy Questions

1. Identify the various sources cited in the article "Marketers Are Sizing Up the Millennials" (on page 86). How does Dionne Searcey attribute information to each of these sources in her article? How effective are Searcey's attributions in helping the reader identify her sources?

2. In "Small Shops Take Pride in Turning Their Backs on Black Friday" (on page 189), Stacy Cowley directly quotes Nan Morningstar. What are the strengths of the use of a direct quote as opposed to a paraphrase? What are the weaknesses?

3. Compare the headlines of "Apple's Biggest Problem? My Mom" (on page 154) and "Spend, Spend, Spend. It's the American Way." (on page 15). Which is a more compelling headline, and why? How could the less compelling headline be changed to better draw the reader's interest?

4. Does Natasha Singer demonstrate the journalistic principle of impartiality in her article "Your Online Attention, Bought in an Instant" (on page 77)? If so, how did she do so? If not, what could Singer have included to make her article more impartial?

5. The article "My Year of No Shopping" (on page 197) is an example of an op-ed. Identify how Ann Patchett's attitude and tone help convey her opinion on the topic.

6. Does "Consumers May Be More Trusting of Ads Than Marketers Think" (on page 151) use multiple sources? What are the strengths of using multiple sources in a journalistic piece? What are the weaknesses of relying heavily on only one or a few sources?

7. "The Economics (and Nostalgia) of Dead Malls" (on page 29) features photographs. What do these photographs add to the article?

8. What is the intention of the article "Living With Less. A Lot Less." (on page 176)? How effectively does it achieve its intended purpose?

9. Analyze the authors' reporting in "Amazon Knows What You Buy. And It's Building a Big Ad Business From It." (on page 96) and "Your Online Attention, Bought in an Instant" (on page 77). Do you think one journalist is more balanced in her reporting than the other? If so, why do you think so?

10. Identify each of the sources in "How Companies Learn Your Secrets" (on page 57) as a primary source or a secondary source. Evaluate the reliability and credibility of each source. How does your evaluation of each source change your perspective on this article?

Citations

All citations in this list are formatted according to the Modern Language Association's (MLA) style guide.

BOOK CITATION

THE NEW YORK TIMES EDITORIAL STAFF. *Consumer Culture: Feeding Capitalism.* New York: New York Times Educational Publishing, 2020.

ONLINE ARTICLE CITATIONS

ALTER, ALEXANDRA. " 'Friday Black' Uses Fantasy and Blistering Satire to Skewer Racism and Consumer Culture." *The New York Times*, 19 Oct. 2018, https://www.nytimes.com/2018/10/19/books/friday-black-nana-kwame -adjei-brenyah-debut-collection.html.

BAJAS, VIKAS. "Before You Buy That T-Shirt." *The New York Times*, 18 May 2013, https://www.nytimes.com/2013/05/19/opinion/sunday/before-you -buy-that-t-shirt.html.

BARK, ED. "Americans as Addicts of Consumerism." *The New York Times*, 12 Apr. 2008, https://www.nytimes.com/2008/04/12/arts/television/12foot.html.

BROOKS, ARTHUR C. "Abundance Without Attachment." *The New York Times*, 12 Dec. 2014, https://www.nytimes.com/2014/12/14/opinion/sunday /arthur-c-brooks-abundance-without-attachment.html.

CASSELMAN, BEN. "Holiday Spending Should Be Strong. And Then?" *The New York Times*, 22 Nov. 2018, https://www.nytimes.com/2018/11/22/business /economy/holiday-retail-spending.html.

CHAYKA, KYLE. "The Oppressive Gospel of 'Minimalism.' " *The New York Times*, 26 July 2016, https://www.nytimes.com/2016/07/31/magazine /the-oppressive-gospel-of-minimalism.html.

COHEN, PATRICIA. "Retail Payrolls Sustain a New Blow as Shopping Habits Shift." *The New York Times*, 7 Apr. 2017, https://www.nytimes.com /2017/04/07/business/economy/jobs-report-retail-employment.html.

CORDRAY, RICHARD. "Let Consumers Sue Companies." *The New York Times*, 22 Aug. 2017, https://www.nytimes.com/2017/08/22/opinion/let-consumers-sue-companies.html.

COWLEY, STACY. "Small Shops Take Pride in Turning Their Backs on Black Friday." *The New York Times*, 25 Nov. 2015, https://www.nytimes.com/2015/11/26/business/small-shops-take-pride-in-turning-their-backs-on-black-friday.html.

CROSS, GARY S. "Joy to the Packaging People." *The New York Times*, 12 Dec. 2014, https://www.nytimes.com/2014/12/13/opinion/joy-to-the-packaging-people.html.

CURRID-HALKETT, ELIZABETH. "What People Buy Where." *The New York Times*, 13 Dec. 2014, https://www.nytimes.com/2014/12/14/opinion/sunday/what-people-buy-where.html.

DAVIDSON, ADAM. "What Nail Polish Sales Tell Us About the Economy." *The New York Times*, 14 Dec. 2011, https://www.nytimes.com/2011/12/18/magazine/adam-davidson-economic-indicators.html.

DUHIGG, CHARLES. "How Companies Learn Your Secrets." *The New York Times*, 16 Feb. 2012, https://www.nytimes.com/2012/02/19/magazine/shopping-habits.html.

FRIEDMAN, VANESSA. "Libraries, Gardens, Museums. Oh, and a Clothing Store." *The New York Times*, 19 Nov. 2018, https://www.nytimes.com/2018/11/19/fashion/shopping-malls-asia.html.

GOOLSBEE, AUSTAN. "How Consumers Can Resist Companies' Market Power." *The New York Times*, 20 July 2018, https://www.nytimes.com/2018/07/20/business/how-consumers-can-resist-companies-market-power.html.

HAYS, CONSTANCE L. "Preaching to Save Shoppers From 'Evil' of Consumerism." *The New York Times*, 1 Jan. 2003, https://www.nytimes.com/2003/01/01/business/preaching-to-save-shoppers-from-evil-of-consumerism.html.

HILL, GRAHAM. "Living With Less. A Lot Less." *The New York Times*, 9 Mar. 2013, https://www.nytimes.com/2013/03/10/opinion/sunday/living-with-less-a-lot-less.html.

KORKKI, PHYLLIS. "Paying With Cash Hurts. That's Also Why It Feels So Good." *The New York Times*, 16 July 2016, https://www.nytimes.com/2016/07/17/business/paying-with-cash-hurts-thats-also-why-it-feels-so-good.html.

KURUTZ, STEVEN. "An Ode to Shopping Malls." *The New York Times*, 26 July

2017, https://www.nytimes.com/2017/07/26/fashion/an-ode-to-shopping-malls.html.

LEWIS, PAUL. "In Buying We Trust; The Foundation of U.S. Consumerism Was Laid in the 18th Century." *The New York Times*, 30 May 1998, https://www.nytimes.com/1998/05/30/arts/in-buying-we-trust-the-foundation-of-us-consumerism-was-laid-in-the-18th-century.html.

NORTH, ANNA. "Should You Have Things?" *The New York Times*, 15 Dec. 2014, https://op-talk.blogs.nytimes.com/2014/12/15/should-you-have-things/.

PATCHETT, ANN. "My Year of No Shopping." *The New York Times*, 15 Dec. 2017, https://www.nytimes.com/2017/12/15/opinion/sunday/shopping-consumerism.html.

QUARTZ, STEVEN, AND ANETTE ASP. "Unequal, Yet Happy." *The New York Times*, 11 Apr. 2015, https://www.nytimes.com/2015/04/12/opinion/sunday/unequal-yet-happy.html.

RICHTEL, MATT. "You Can't Take It With You, but You Still Want More." *The New York Times*, 4 Jan. 2014, https://www.nytimes.com/2014/01/05/business/you-cant-take-it-with-you-but-you-still-want-more.html.

ROOSE, KEVIN. "Apple's Biggest Problem? My Mom." *The New York Times*, 5 Jan. 2019, https://www.nytimes.com/2019/01/05/technology/apple-iphone-replacement-mom.html.

ROSENBLUM, STEPHANIE. "But Will It Make You Happy?" *The New York Times*, 7 Aug. 2010, https://www.nytimes.com/2010/08/08/business/08consume.html.

SCHONBRUN, ZACH. "Consumers May Be More Trusting of Ads Than Marketers Think." *The New York Times*, 30 July 2017, https://www.nytimes.com/2017/07/30/business/media/consumers-may-be-more-trusting-of-ads-than-marketers-think.html.

SCHWARTZ, NELSON D. "Credit Cards Encourage Extra Spending as the Cash Habit Fades Away." *The New York Times*, 25 Mar. 2016, https://www.nytimes.com/2016/03/27/your-money/credit-cards-encourages-extra-spending-as-the-cash-habit-fades-away.html.

SCHWARTZ, NELSON D. "The Economics (and Nostalgia) of Dead Malls." *The New York Times*, 3 Jan. 2015, https://www.nytimes.com/2015/01/04/business/the-economics-and-nostalgia-of-dead-malls.html.

SEARCEY, DIONNE. "Marketers Are Sizing Up the Millennials." *The New York Times*, 21 Aug. 2014, https://www.nytimes.com/2014/08/22/business/marketers-are-sizing-up-the-millennials-as-the-new-consumer-model.html.

SHILLER, ROBERT J. "Spend, Spend, Spend. It's the American Way." *The New York Times*, 14 Jan. 2012, https://www.nytimes.com/2012/01/15/business/consumer-spending-as-an-american-virtue.html.

SINGER, NATASHA. "Your Online Attention, Bought in an Instant." *The New York Times*, 17 Nov. 2012, https://www.nytimes.com/2012/11/18/technology/your-online-attention-bought-in-an-instant-by-advertisers.html.

TABUCHI, HIROKO. "Black Friday Shopping Shifts Online as Stores See Less Foot Traffic." *The New York Times*, 27 Nov. 2015, https://www.nytimes.com/2015/11/28/business/black-friday-shopping-shifts-online-as-stores-see-less-foot-traffic.html.

UNDERHILL, PACO. "Walmart Can't Escape Clutter. Can You?" *The New York Times*, 19 Dec. 2015, https://www.nytimes.com/2015/12/20/opinion/sunday/walmart-cant-escape-clutter-can-you.html.

VALENTINO-DEVRIES, JENNIFER. "How E-Commerce Sites Manipulate You Into Buying Things You May Not Want." *The New York Times*, 24 June 2019, https://www.nytimes.com/2019/06/24/technology/e-commerce-dark-patterns-psychology.html.

WALK-MORRIS, TATIANA. "Blacks Are Challenged to Buy From Black-Owned Businesses to Close Gap." *The New York Times*, 15 Nov. 2015, https://www.nytimes.com/2015/11/16/business/blacks-are-challenged-to-buy-from-black-owned-businesses-to-close-gap.html.

WALKER, ROB. "Digital Culture, Meet Analog Fever." *The New York Times*, 28 Nov. 2015, https://www.nytimes.com/2015/11/29/opinion/sunday/digital-culture-meet-analog-fever.html.

WEISE, KAREN. "Amazon Knows What You Buy. And It's Building a Big Ad Business From It." *The New York Times*, 20 Jan. 2019, https://www.nytimes.com/2019/01/20/technology/amazon-ads-advertising.html.

WILLIAMS, ALEX. "Buying Into the Green Movement." *The New York Times*, 1 July 2007, https://www.nytimes.com/2007/07/01/fashion/01green.html.

ZANE, J. PEDER. "In Pursuit of Taste, en Masse." *The New York Times*, 11 Feb. 2013, https://www.nytimes.com/2013/02/12/business/connoisseurship-expands-beyond-high-art-and-classical-music.html.

Index

This book is current up until the time of printing. For the most up-to-date reporting, visit www.nytimes.com.